monsoonbooks

RICE WINE AND DANCING GIRLS

Wong Seng Chow is a self-described "shy, introverted Asian who cannot drink"—though there are differing opinions on this.

After retiring from a successful career in corporate life, Wong decided to pursue his long-time passion for travel and writing. The confluence of these two interests led, of course, to his becoming a freelance journalist.

His travel-related articles have appeared in the in-flight magazines of Malaysia Airlines and SilkAir.

In this, his first published book, Wong Seng Chow weaves an entertaining tale based on his father's life as an itinerant cinema manager, and, in so doing, uncovers the man behind the patriarch and travelling movie maven.

T0150028

These are the stories my father never told me.

RICE WINE AND DANCING GIRLS

Wong Seng Chow

monsoon

monsoonbooks

Published in 2008
by Monsoon Books Pte Ltd
52 Telok Blangah Road
#03-05 Telok Blangah House
Singapore 098829
www.monsoonbooks.com.sg

ISBN: 978-981-08-1083-2

Copyright © Wong Seng Chow, 2008
The moral right of the author has been asserted.

All rights reserved. No part of this publication may be
reproduced, stored in a retrieval system, or transmitted,
in any form or by any means without the prior written
permission of the publisher, nor be otherwise circulated
in any form of binding or cover other than that in which
it is published and without a similar condition being
imposed on the subsequent purchaser.

Cover and inside photos © Wong Seng Chow

Wong, Seng Chow.
Rice wine and dancing girls / Wong Seng Chow. – Singapore : Monsoon
Books, 2008.
p. cm.
ISBN-13 : 978-981-08-1083-2 (pbk.)
1. Wong, Kee Hung. 2. Motion picture theater managers – Singapore
– Biography. 3. Motion picture theater managers – Malaysia
– Biography. 4. Cathay (Organization) – History. I. Title.
PN1998.3
791.43092 -- dc22   OCN243732698

Printed in Singapore

12 11 10 09 08   1 2 3 4 5 6 7 8 9

In memory of Bong Kai Hong
Born in the year of the Metal Pig
Died in the year of the Fire Pig

Contents

Preface

"Looking back all these years, events of my life flashed through my mind like a cinemascopic [sic] *picture."*

These were the opening lines on the first page of a slim exercise book, written in the neat, cursive handwriting of my father. Undoubtedly, his life story contains all the ingredients of a celluloid drama: a young man shackled to his hometown, finds redemption and renewal when he is propelled into the big, wide world filled with a kaleidoscope of characters, ranging from movie stars and governors to gangsters and headhunters. Armed with just a foldable camp bed and mosquito net, his wanderings take him into unfamiliar and sometimes dangerous territories.

Some of the anecdotes relating to his service with Cathay have already been retold in the organisation's 55th anniversary limited-edition coffee-table book (*Cathay: 55 Years of Cinema*, by Lim Kay Tong and Yiu Tong Chai, 1991) whilst a broad sweep of his life, from childhood to retirement from Cathay in 1978, has been recorded by the Oral History section of the National Archives of Singapore in a series of interviews in the last quarter of 2005. Given the opportunity, he would regale friends and visitors with vignettes of the years spent as a roving cinema manager in the fifties and sixties. This was the most colourful period of his life and one that he was proudest of. However, as a child I was too young to understand; as a teenager too rebellious to care; and later as an adult too busy to listen. Thankfully, he kept copious, albeit scattered notes—some handwritten, some typewritten—of those eventful days. What is presented here is based on salient episodes of his life woven against the backdrop of historical events. It is the tale of a belated quest for self-worth by a man with a character flaw. Here, then, are the stories that my father never told me.

Wong Seng Chow

Prologue

The old man seated in the wheelchair pulls himself forward with a shuffling motion of his bare feet. Gliding across the living room, he stops in front of the television set sitting on the lower alcove of the display cabinet and reaches for the battered remote control with his mottled hand. His thick spectacles can no longer compensate for his deteriorating vision, making it difficult for him to make out the tiny lettering on the remote without the aid of a magnifying glass. In fact, he has two: a standard lightweight magnifying lens with a plastic grip commonly found at stationery stores, and a heavier one of craftsman-quality that came with a varnished wooden handle and its own zip-up pouch. His son had searched high and low to get him the second, more powerful instrument as a present for his 95th birthday. But he doesn't make use of either one of them for the task at hand. Instead, his thumb travels over the familiar series of bumps on the remote's stained surface, as if following the markings of a treasure map, until he locates the correct button and presses it. The screen flashes to life with a crisp rasp of electrons and he turns up the volume to mask the depressing silence wrapped around him. It's not that he lives alone but he's left mostly to himself by the other members of the family, the lives of his son, daughter-in-law and two grandchildren swirling around him like kites caught in a whirlwind of activities that he cannot be part of, whilst he remains rooted to a past that they have little interest in. There was a time when he had his wife to talk to…although it couldn't really be called a conversation when he had to constantly repeat and explain things to her because she was hard of hearing and showing signs of dementia as well. Still, she had provided a focus for his attention.

Friends and relatives who visited him marvelled at his obvious devotion to his wife, which was why her sporadic outbursts of resentment over his constant fussing were incomprehensible to him. But she had passed away three years before and his few surviving friends were locked in their own struggle with old-age infirmities, restricting contact between them to well-worn pleasantries over the phone. Such conversations lasted less than a minute, during which he would interject with phrases like "You take care, thank you," inviting closure for fear that their next sentence might be consumed by an awkward silence, revealing the emptiness of their lives.

Whilst the telephone provides a connection to his friends and a fleeting uplift of spirit, the television marks the passage of time through its weekly cycle of programmes. Both offer a break from the pattern of his days that seem like a blur of raindrops, each one the same as the next. Sometimes he sits motionless in front of the screen, as if absorbed, staring with rheumy eyes at the moving images and listening to dialogue that he no longer consciously registers. During moments like these his mind slips into a fugue that transports him to another time and place.

Soft Drinks and Dancing Girls

Following the Japanese surrender in August 1945, life in the British colonies of Malaya and Singapore slowly returned to normal. By 1946 public utility services had been fully restored and the strong world demand for tin and rubber helped the Malayan economy along a rather uneven road to recovery; problems like food shortages still persisted, which in turn caused widespread strikes calling for higher wages to deal with escalating food prices. However, this background of turbulence did not dampen the hopes of those who were intent on rebuilding their lives after having emerged from the vicissitudes of the Second World War.

Pebble

I sat at the usual place in the coffee shop, as was my habit these past few weeks, and watched the town folk of Seremban rouse themselves for a new day. The smell of toast and corn-roasted coffee hung in the air as the morning tide of customers rolled in for their sugar and caffeine boost. Across from me at the next table, a man grumbled to his companion about the cost of eggs as he tilted his saucer and slurped down a runny yellow-white concoction laced with soya sauce and pepper. The scraping sound of wooden stools being pushed back announced the departure of an earlier group of customers, whose places were snapped up by new arrivals even before the breakfast debris could be cleared from the table. The shop buzzed with lively chatter, reflecting the general post-war optimism that things would soon be back to how they'd been before. But returning to my normal life was not what I had in mind.

I was a teacher before the war. My alma mater, St Paul's Institution, had been steadily acquiring a reputation for excellence in academic and sporting achievements, and though it had expanded its facilities to accommodate the rising number of enrolments, the school continued to face a shortage of staff. I lacked the credentials to become a bona fide teacher but the Brothers of the school took into account that I was an outstanding former "Paulian" student, so they accepted me as a lay teacher and assigned me to teach English to the primary classes. I was paid $60 a month (the currency in use at that time was the Straits dollar which later became the Malaya and British Borneo dollar) that I guessed was commensurate with my lowly status as a student-teacher. I might have just been able to squeeze out a simple, carefree bachelor's life on that paltry sum if not for the fact that I was already a married man with two kids. In order to support my family I had to give private tuition on the side as well.

However, I still found the time to be with my friends and regularly dropped by at the local recreation club, leaving the children under the care of my wife. Such was the routine of my life before it was abruptly disrupted by the Japanese occupation of Malaya and Singapore in 1942. The military administration set up to govern the conquered territories decreed that English could no longer be taught as a subject, and schools were forced to adopt a Japanese-dictated curriculum. I had no wish to be part of their propaganda machinery disguised as education and resigned from my post. To make matters worse, parents stopped sending their children to my home for English tuition for fear of punishment, leaving me without any source of income and at a loss as to how I was going to feed myself and my family.

One of my closest friends, Chen, also left his job as a result of the war but for a different reason. After obtaining his degree from America, Chen went to work for an engineering firm in Singapore. He had barely established himself in the company when news broke that the Japanese had landed in north-west Malaya and were sweeping down the peninsula. Fearing that he might be stranded in Singapore, Chen bolted back to his family home in Seremban, a move that seemed to defy logic since he was leaving a heavily defended city and heading north towards a vulnerable town in the path of the Japanese advance. Nevertheless, Chen felt that he would be relatively safer in his hometown, far removed from what he anticipated to be an inevitable arena of bloody conflict—the strategic island port of Singapore and last bastion of Allied resistance. It proved a prudent decision.

The destruction of the bridge link between Singapore and the mainland only temporarily delayed the expected Japanese assault. A week of fierce fighting followed before the British finally surrendered on the fateful day of 15th February 1942. Coincidentally, it was also the first day of the Lunar Year of the Horse but instead of enjoying festive celebrations, the ethnic Chinese in Singapore found themselves the target of Japanese retribution for providing substantial charitable aid to China, a country still struggling against Japanese imperialism in the ongoing Second Sino-Japanese War.

Back in Seremban, the town folk adjusted to their new situation after the initial panic, that saw children and loved ones being packed off to villages in the jungle or hiding in nearby caves, and attempted to carry on with their lives as best as they could. Chen failed to find work relevant to his background as an engineer so he ventured into business instead. With some help, he set up a transport company that delivered rubber from the plantations to the port warehouses for ongoing shipment. Knowing of my plight, he recruited me into the company as a clerk. I was grateful to be working again, having been unemployed for several months, but my relief was short-lived. I discovered that I wasn't that much better off than before as my meagre clerical wage barely paid for the inflated war-time prices of basic commodities. Rice, salt and sugar, items previously taken for granted because they had been readily and cheaply available, were now hard to come by. Once again I was forced to look for ways to supplement my income, which was how I ended up moonlighting as a croupier in one of the many gambling stalls that populated the amusement fair behind Lemon Street.

The fair was a permanent fixture in the Seremban landscape; it existed before the arrival of the Japanese invaders and remained open for business under Japanese rule as if nothing had happened. The assortment of brightly lit stalls drew people in nightly like moths to a flame. They came to mingle with the crowd, browse the wares on display, sample some titbits and perhaps try their luck at one of the game stalls. But most of all, the residents of Seremban came because it gave them a sense of normalcy. The gambling stalls in particular were kept busy by the regular punters who reasoned that the Japanese presence was not something they could do much about anyway, and continued to pursue their passion with an even greater fervour.

I manned a *pai kow* gambling table. The game is related to Baccarat but uses domino tiles instead of cards. The tiles are shuffled and stacked into a wall four tiles high by eight tiles long. Each player receives a stack of four tiles that are split into pairs of a high hand and a low hand to be compared against the banker's set. I was familiar enough with the mechanics of the game having been exposed to it from young when I used to watch my mother play whilst clinging to her *samfoo* dress. As indicated by its name—which means to "make nine"—winning hands are those that have domino pips adding up closest to the number nine. However, this apparently simple ranking is complicated by special winning combinations that are given fanciful labels such as "heaven", "earth", "man", "goose" and "flower", to give some examples. Typically, there would be cries of jubilation from the punters when they won but more often than not they were hunched in sullen concentration, riffling through their carefully hoarded savings of pre-war currency, which was worth far more than the official Japanese "banana" notes, to fund future bets that would hopefully recoup their losses. Such intense desperation made me glad that I was on the other side of the table earning a fixed per diem wage as a croupier. Not that I didn't gamble—I was fond of "washing mahjong tiles" with friends at the club— but this was neither the time nor place to risk money I could ill afford to lose.

When the war ended, Chen no longer had a reason to remain in Seremban and headed straight back to Singapore to resurrect his nascent career. Unlike him, I wasn't anxious to pick up where I'd left off. Somehow, a sense of discontent had been awakened in me and I had no desire to return to the teaching fold. When I recalled the years I spent eking out a living on the fringe of academia, I wondered what would have happened if not for the interruption of the war: would I have continued to sleepwalk through life as a lay teacher and part-time tutor? I didn't know the answer. What I did know was that the momentum of circumstances in the last few years compelled me to move on—like a pebble that had been dislodged and forced to tumble towards fresh ground in its search for a new equilibrium. It wasn't going to be easy with my limited qualifications and no other work experience beyond teaching and clerical work. Citing my skill as a *pai kow* croupier would have added some colour but little extra value to my resume. Not that I bothered to send out any resumes for I relied on my network of hometown friends to spread the word and like the spiders I used to catch when I was a boy, I spun my web and waited.

The crowd at the coffee shop was beginning to ebb away as individually, or in small groups, people drained the dregs from their cups and left for work. I watched the world slide by, idly stirring the sticky condensed milk submerged at the bottom of my cup before sipping my thick sweet coffee. A sudden slap on my back snapped me out of my reverie and, turning around, I saw that it was Yin, an old schoolmate. Yin sat down and signalled to the coffee-shop boy for his drink.

"Kee Hung, I hear you're looking for a job. Got tired of drilling grammar to the greenies?" I winced for I had previously done part-time clerical work for Yin at the Negri Sembilan Aerated Water Company—or NSAW for short—before taking up teaching; I hoped that he wasn't using this opportunity to rope me back to that same old job. I was on the verge of explaining to him that I was after something a bit more stable and perhaps more rewarding when Yin surprised me with his offer. It was serendipity! He was scouting for someone to fill the position of chief clerk at NSAW. The incumbent was getting on in age and Yin wanted a younger, more alert replacement. The job entailed greater administrative and clerical responsibilities than what I had been used to and even though I was fairly confident that I would be able carry them out, I expressed cautious interest initially. But any doubts that were lingering at the back of mind melted away like a one-cent flavoured ice-ball on a scorching hot day when Yin mentioned the pay—it was twice what I used to earn as a lay teacher!

"When do I start?" I enquired as I hurriedly fished for coins to pay for the drink that the boy plonked down in front of my friend and future boss.

Mirror Moon

Yin was formerly a lawyer's clerk. It was his father-in-law Goh, who ran NSAW together with his adopted son Ah-Kow, the latter being the mastermind of the formulae and mixes for the Lemonade, Orange, Ice Cream Soda and other soft drink flavours that they produced. When the old man passed away, Yin took over the reins of the company.

As chief clerk, I was in charge of office administration and had the assistance of a bookkeeper as well as an office boy to run errands. With the memory of hardships shared during the war still fresh in everyone's mind, the previous chief clerk was retained in an advisory capacity—albeit on a token salary—but was content to remain very much in the background. It was during this period at NSAW that I first met Ah-Yong, a fellow employee. Fate would entwine the threads of our lives again in the near future.

The soft drinks factory was located at the junction of Setul Road and Temiang Road and occupied a sizeable piece of land that it shared with a large one-storey wooden building. The latter housed the Negri Sembilan Cabaret that operated from eight o'clock in the evening until midnight on weekdays but closed an hour later on Saturdays. Sunday was a day of rest. The so-called cabaret was really a dance hall boasting a six-piece resident band led by a Filipino pianist by the name of Adrian. He and his family—a wife and teenaged son—had living quarters in the compound next to the premises, presumably as part of his terms of employment but more likely as a concession to the fact that he was lame in one leg.

The cabaret also employed at least a dozen dance hostesses, comprising mostly Chinese girls and a few Eurasians. They would sit patiently on the chairs lining the opposite sides of the hall, waiting to dance with patrons in exchange for coupons. Each coupon was worth a dollar and they were sold in booklets of five coupons. The girls earned a commission based on the number of dance coupons that they redeemed with the cabaret at the end of the week. Naturally, the prettier dance hostesses were more popular and raked in higher earnings. My intimate knowledge about the dance hall's operation did not stem from frequent patronage as a customer, but from performing my duties there as a supervisor. As it turned out, the cabaret was operated by NSAW, and Ah-Kow would don his cabaret-manager hat after sunset. So when I was asked to pitch in and lend a hand, it seemed like the natural thing to do.

Supervising a cabaret in the evenings was in sharp contrast to my mundane daytime clerical work. On quieter nights at the beginning of the week I could relax and enjoy listening to Adrian, who was an excellent pianist, performing with his band whilst the scattering of local customers twirled and sashayed across the spacious dance floor with their chosen partners.

The atmosphere took a much livelier turn towards the end of the week, with the hall filling up with noisy British servicemen intent on having a good time. Their high spirits, fuelled by alcohol, would inevitably ignite tempers sparked by a perceived insult, competition over a girl, or a host of minor reasons that didn't make sense in the sober light of the following day. Although I have a fairly large build and my height of six foot allowed me to look squarely in the eyes of most British servicemen, I figured being a bouncer wasn't part of my extended duties. Whenever trouble erupted, I would dial for the Military Police, shouting over the phone in order to be heard above the background din of a drunken brawl whilst keeping an eye out for the wayward trajectory of bottles and glasses flying about!

I didn't mind doubling up as a cabaret supervisor even though I wasn't paid any over-time wages. I saw it as returning the favour to Yin for giving me the position of chief clerk based on friendship and a handshake. The months flew by as I settled into a routine of dealing with soft drinks by day and dancing girls by night. Before I knew it I was entering my second year with NSAW and it seemed that I had found my niche. Unfortunately, events were once again conspiring to unsettle my life.

Competition in the aerated water market was heating up, with NSAW having to contend with a host of other manufacturers as well as the threat from the rapidly expanding Fraser & Neave. In trying to manage both the soft drinks factory and the cabaret, Yin was beginning to encounter cash-flow problems. This, in turn, affected the NSAW staff whose salaries were either delayed or only partially paid. Yin wasn't a heartless man but he was desperately juggling his finances to keep his two business operations afloat. It was always his intention to pay back in full what he owed in wages…when things got better. Since my income just about covered my expenses, the vagaries in salary disbursement often left me short of cash, and my struggle to make ends meet was accompanied by a dizzy feeling of déjà vu. Only this time I couldn't slip out to moonlight as a croupier because I was already fully occupied as a supervisor at the cabaret.

There is a mythical belief that a man at the age of thirty-five is at the prime of his life cycle. In adolescence a boy struggles with his transition to manhood and is faced with the question of identity: "Who am I?" On reaching thirty-five years of age, he takes stock of his accomplishments by asking the question: "What am I?" I was already thirty-six. Joining NSAW had seemed like a good move and I trusted that, with diligence and hard work, I would progress within the company.

The reality was that both Yin and Ah-Kow were firmly at the helm of what was essentially a family business, and I had no prospect of advancing further. Wishful thinking, buoyed by my eagerness to assume the post of chief clerk, had clouded my judgment and when I eventually realised that I'd stepped into a dead-end job, I quietly tucked away my fettered hopes and tried to make the best of it. After all, it was still better than teaching. However, the pressure of unpaid bills steadily piling up broke the dam of my equanimity. Accepting the status quo of the company's management hierarchy was one thing, but with the very future of the company being threatened and no end in sight to erratic salary payments, I couldn't help but sink into a pensive mood. I still continued to faithfully discharge all my duties, although the additional task of being a supervisor at the cabaret now seemed like a chore, and even Adrian's tickling of the ivories failed to revive my spirits.

One night I made some excuse to leave the dance hall before

closing time. It was too late to head to the local recreation club to meet up with friends and I was reluctant to go straight home. Wandering aimlessly, I came to an open field that doubled as a car park by day and was shunned as a deserted lot by the distant streetlamps by night. Guided mainly by moonlight, I stubbornly picked my way across the uneven ground, pausing midway to take a deep breath. I glanced up at the refulgent orb that hung suspended in the night sky and found it staring back at me, its ethereal radiance illuminating my inner turmoil. The feeling of haplessness was exacerbated by the vacuum in my relationship with my wife. It had been an arranged marriage, the machination of parents who thought they were doing what was best for everyone even if that meant sacrificing the feelings of the two people directly affected. I suspect that my failure to harvest the security of the future for the family because I'd dropped out of college, and my subsequent inability to secure a decent job, prompted my father to cash in on my eligibility as an unmarried twenty-four-year-old man. He brokered a deal that involved a handsome dowry from the owner of a Chinese medicine hall in a neighbouring town, who was eager to see his twenty-three-year-old daughter wedded.

Whilst the ceremony that took place followed customary Chinese rituals, the fashion was distinctly Western; I was sombre in my dark suit, wing-collared white shirt and black bow tie whilst she was stiff in her ankle-length, high-collared white wedding gown crowned by a cloche with a trailing tulle veil. She looked trapped in her bridal garment, just as she was trapped by her circumstances; denied a proper education, she was restricted in her options of what she could do with her life and a touchy temperament did little to endear her to potential suitors. As for me, I was robbed of volition to resist by the milieu that shaped and defined me. To oppose the marriage was not only going against my father's wishes, it was also a rejection of my place in Seremban society ... it just seemed easier to go along with the whole thing. The marriage was consummated and to the delight of my parents, they were presented with two grandchildren—a boy, followed by a girl two years later. I have no doubt that there are many examples of arranged marriages where, over time, couples develop a genuine affection if not mutual respect for each other, but this was not the case with us and it was only through our children that we could bridge the gulf of our incompatibility.

My brooding turned to comparing myself to friends who were doing well in their chosen line of work; Chen had branched off with two partners to set up a civil engineering and general construction firm in Singapore whilst a childhood playmate, Ng, had become a successful contractor in Seremban. In contrast, I always seemed to just get by. Such things had never really bothered me before. As long as I provided for the family and could enjoy the company of my many friends, I was relaxed about my lot in life. Why grasp for the moon when you know it is out of reach?

Still, I realised I wasn't getting any younger and I shuddered to think that I might end up grasping at straws instead. The irony of it struck me. My attempt to improve my situation merely sent me on a box-step waltz that brought me back to square one, and whilst it wasn't my fault that things turned out the way they did at NSAW, it didn't make me feel any better. Weary of all this inutile introspection, I decided to head home.

Deus Ex Machina

The end of 1947 saw Dato Loke Wan Tho, whose name is synonymous with Cathay, ready to roll out his aggressive expansion plans. The title "Dato" was only conferred on Loke Wan Tho in 1962 but I've always fondly and respectfully remembered him as Dato Loke, whilst at the same time, I use the term Cathay[1] for convenience even though the company was not known as "Cathay Organisation" until 1959. His general manager, the scholarly looking Ede, was exploring the towns all over Malaya with the view of acquiring cinemas for the organisation, or at least buildings that could be turned into cinemas. Ede made a stop in Seremban and after making enquiries was directed to Yin. As luck would have it, there was a large, unused wooden shed in the NSAW compound and Ede met up with Yin to negotiate for the lease of this building with the intention of converting it into

---

[1] Similarly, "Shaw" is used in place of "Shaw Brothers" or "Shaw Organisation".

a cinema hall. Yin was more than happy to sign an agreement. I couldn't help but be aware of what was going on and banking on the fact that Cathay would need a manager for its Seremban cinema (to be called the Odeon) when it was ready, I did something I'd never done before in my life: I approached a stranger for a job. It was a desperate move on my part but then I reasoned that there was no harm in asking. After patiently listening to my earnest pitch for the post of manager in the future Odeon, Ede advised me to submit a formal application to the Cathay head office in Singapore. I took heart that he hadn't rejected me outright. With that consoling thought, I mailed my application and crossed my fingers.

Even though I knew it would take time for my letter to be delivered and processed, I checked my mail every day. A week crawled by, then another, with each passing day bleeding hope from me till I was left pallid at the ignominy of not just being rejected but ignored as well. The cosmic jester must have been at work for the reply arrived the moment I stopped waiting for it. Tearing open the envelope, I nervously unfolded the single piece of paper; the neatly typed words jumped up from the page and threw me on an emotional roller coaster of both elation and despondency. The missive tersely explained that all new cinema managers had to undergo training in Singapore first, and Cathay was pleased to inform me that I'd been accepted as a management trainee at the start of the following year—just a few months away.

That was the good news. The bad news was that I would only be receiving my training allowances after I'd begun my internship. In other words, I had to bear all initial expenses myself. I didn't know whether to laugh or cry, for surely I was the victim of that same cosmic jester who had toyed with my patience, to have the prospect of a new career cruelly dangled just out of my reach knowing that I couldn't even pay for the train fare to Singapore!

I am not what you might call a religious man. Although I'd attended a Catholic mission school, I did not subscribe to its faith. I observe the Chinese traditions because it's part of my cultural heritage but I don't harbour any strong beliefs in Buddhism or Taoism. If anything, you could say I veer towards aspects of Confucianism. In Cantonese, my spiritual orientation would be labelled as "half sky hung", meaning that I'm stranded between heaven and earth—being neither here nor there—which pretty much summed up my predicament. As such, I did not pray to any deity or make votive offerings for my salvation but I did bemoan my situation to friends, making light of it to hide my disappointment. One such friend with whom I shared the story of my aborted attempt to join Cathay was Ng, the contractor.

Ng and I went back a long way, having known each other since we were seven years old. We used to fly kites together, assembling them from bamboo strips and paper, and would reap gleeful delight to see our flimsy contraptions soar and dance their aerial jig. Kite flying was a favourite activity of mine until it turned gladiatorial when older boys in the neighbourhood started using strings treated with glass to cut the lines of other kites. Faced with the repeated fate of having our strings severed and our kites tumble helplessly out of control, we retired from the scene. My father got angry when he found out and decided to give me a chance to fight back by similarly coating my kite string with glass. The process involved pounding glass bottles; boiling gum; soaking the kite string in the gum; running the string though the glass powder and finally laying out the string to dry. Unfortunately, he wasn't very good at it. The glass powder stuck in clumps and the weight of the glue-soaked string tended to drag the kite down.

So Ng and I turned to collecting picture cards instead. They were usually included as inserts in cigarette packs and originally depicted famous Chinese generals, but later featured male and female film stars. We would scavenge for discarded cigarette packs, hoping to find the cards still inside. Duplicate cards in our possession were traded, or used to play a game with other boys where we would all crouch behind a line marked on the ground about five feet from a wall and then see who could flick his card nearest to the wall. The winner would claim all the cards in play. It wasn't as challenging as flying a kite but at least we were still having fun.

Ng listened with a sympathetic ear and when I was done playing the raconteur, he dug into his trousers and pulled out a brick of banknotes secured by rubber bands. It wasn't unusual to see him carry wads of money since he often had to settle payments with his labourers directly. Slipping off the rubber bands, Ng peeled off a number of bills and pressed them into my hand saying, "This is for you." I was flabbergasted since I was simply sharing my woes without any ulterior motives. Nevertheless, Ng had generously bankrolled my internship in Singapore to the tune of a hundred dollars, an amount that was almost equivalent to my salary (if I was lucky enough to receive it) at NSAW. Whenever I look back on this episode in my life, I am reminded of the classic movie plots where the hero's quest, stalled by capricious circumstances, is given fresh impetus by some unexpected and timely external intervention. I was no hero but Ng's largesse was unexpected and timely. I pocketed the cash with a murmur of thanks and promised to repay him as soon as I could. He merely smiled and patted me on the shoulder.

"Let's get this straight, Kee Hung. It's not a loan. It's a going-away present." Ng's paragon gesture of friendship was to be indelibly etched in my mind, and it was only ten years later that I had the chance to repay him in kind ... but that's another story.

And so in January 1948 I boarded a train to Singapore, taking along with me one suitcase, a foldable camp bed, a mosquito net, my tennis racket and the conviction that I would be able to hold my head high when I returned to manage the Odeon in Seremban. Little did I realise that I was embarking on a one-way trip.

EPISODE 2

Mayhem and Manhunt

Post-war Malaya came directly under the British Military Administration (BMA), who pushed for the formation of the Malayan Union in order to facilitate the governing of the British territories in Malaya (by merging the various Malay states and parts of the Straits Settlement into a single political entity) and also to pave the way for eventual self-government in the region. The Union was created in 1946 but while it was political progress in principle, it was not workable in detail and was replaced two years later in February 1948 by the Federation of Malaya. The stability of the newly formed Federation immediately came under threat from the increasingly violent Communist agitation that culminated in the murder of three European plantation managers, prompting the authorities to declare the Malayan Emergency in June 1948.

By August of the same year, the BMA was cracking down hard on the Malayan Communist Party (MCP) members and their associates; those who had not already been arrested or deported fled to the jungles to re-organise themselves as an anti-British guerrilla force.

In Good Company

Being a pragmatic person, I chose to conserve my funds by asking Chen, who was now living at Bournemouth Road on the east coast of Singapore, whether I could put up with him. "Yah, Kee Hung, no problem staying with me, there's plenty of room. Don't know whether you can 'put up with me' though," he quipped. We were both thrilled to be able to spend time together and spent many a night reminiscing about the mischief we'd got up to in our younger days.

Five guys and a "Baby Austin".

"Do you remember our trip to Singapore?"

Chen flashed a grin and gave a theatrical groan. "How could I forget?"

It was during one of the holiday breaks when, together with three other school friends, we decided to visit Singapore instead of making our usual pilgrimage to the seaside town of Port Dickson. Chen persuaded his father to lend him the keys to his pride and joy, an Austin 7 convertible which was a popular British car first introduced in 1922. Nicknamed the "Baby Austin", it was a light, small sporty vehicle that seated four comfortably but was a squeeze for the five of us. It lacked a boot so all our luggage had to be strapped to the back where the spare wheel would normally have been affixed. Loaded to the brim, the Austin's 747cc engine still managed to boost us up to a reasonable speed as we motored our way to Singapore.

Fortunately it didn't rain. Although the car could be fitted with a collapsible top and side curtains, we preferred the exhilarating feel of the wind in our hair and the sun on our faces, letting out boyish whoops of excitement whenever the spindly wheels of the car went over a hump or pothole. It was a long, tiring drive requiring several rest stops, but we arrived safely in Singapore despite some harrowing moments when we negotiated, with more exuberance than caution, the narrow winding roads that hugged the steep slopes of rugged hills.

The next couple of days were spent exploring the city—which

impressed us as being bigger and busier than Seremban—and driving round the island taking in the sights. It was on the eve of our departure, and in the midst of packing for an early-morning checkout we discovered we were collectively short of cash. This set off a frantic verbal crossfire as everyone tried to speak at the same time: "Are you sure you counted correctly?" "I told you we shouldn't have splurged on the seafood dinner!" "Everyone check your pockets for loose change!"

"What are we going to do?" someone wailed.

Despite having saved on accommodation by cramming ourselves into a single room in a cheap hotel, we'd neglected to take into account incidental expenses and now didn't have enough money to both tank up on petrol for our return trip and settle outstanding bills as well.

Nobody remembers who finally came up with the plan, but everyone readily agreed to it. Thus in the wee hours of the morning, with the city still draped in darkness, the five of us crept stealthily out of the hotel and tiptoed towards the adjacent parking lot. Slowly and quietly we rolled the Austin past the night watchman, snoring on his makeshift cot, onto the street and after that continued to push it some distance away. As soon as we had secured our luggage, Chen gingerly started the car but in the stillness of pre-dawn, the sound of the engine coughing to life amplified into a lion's roar. Fearing that the noise had startled the night watchman into wakefulness, Chen slammed hard on the gas pedal even before the rest of us had properly seated ourselves, causing everyone to pile on top of each other in a tangled mass of limbs as the car sped down the deserted street.

When we finally made it back to Seremban, Chen was aghast to find unsightly dents in the rear of the Austin! He had promised to return the car to his father in good condition and had been quite careful to avoid mishaps with other road users. But he never imagined that the heavy suitcases would be the cause of bruised bodywork as a result of their constant knocking against the car during the round trip of three hundred miles or so. His father was most displeased to say the least but nevertheless, continued to

In the wee hours of the morning we rolled the Austin 7 onto the street.

indulge his eldest son by loaning him the car, albeit only for the shorter trips to Port Dickson.

I had to report for work at Cathay Building located at Dhoby Ghaut. The place was all new to me as it had been built in the late 1930s and I had not been back in Singapore for quite a while. The colonial-style building with a bakery that previously occupied the plot of land had been replaced by an impressive sixteen-storey structure that dominated the cityscape. It was the tallest building in Singapore and it housed a hotel, restaurant and cinema. Inevitably, this architectural landmark became a focal point during the war years and was variously used as a broadcasting centre, air-raid shelter, and operations control centre. The Japanese commandeered it for their military information and propaganda departments during the Occupation, and after the war it briefly served as the headquarters for the Supreme Allied Commander, Admiral Lord Mountbatten.

At Cathay, I was joined by another trainee called Lim. The first thing I noticed about him was the long scar on one of his arms that I surmised must have been the result of an accident but I thought it was impolite to ask since we had only just been introduced to each other. We had to undergo a couple of weeks of training before being given our individual assignments. It was more like an orientation really, for we basically shadowed Verdayne, the manager of the Cathay Singapore and a veteran of the company, mentally noting his explanations: about ticketing procedures; the delivery and storage of film reels; how the projectors worked; staff administration; keeping the halls clean and a host of other details involved in the smooth and efficient running of a cinema. One day, during our rounds, we discovered another side to the gentlemanly, white-haired Verdayne when he displayed his pugilistic skills, honed in the boxing ring during his younger days, by peremptorily dealing with rowdies who were making a nuisance of themselves in a crowd of ticket buyers. So it was to my wry amusement when I found out that not only was I rubbing shoulders with an ex-boxer but an ex-soldier as well, for as I got to know Lim better, I found out that he had served with the Kuomintang army and the scar was a souvenir from a sword slash. Of course, I had no inkling at that time that I would soon be sharing a room with an ex-guerrilla fighter!

At the end of our crash course on cinema management, Lim was sent to the venerable Pavilion in Kuala Lumpur whilst I was assigned to Batu Pahat in the western part of the state of Johore.

Lonely Rock

Why the town was called Chiseled Rock was a mystery but that was the literal translation of the town's name Batu Pahat. I didn't care much for mysteries and even less for the place. My heart sank when I learnt of my posting for I had nurtured a naïve hope all this while that I would be sent back to Seremban on completion of my training. But Cathay had made no such promise and in any case, the position in Seremban had already been filled. Aside from spending two years in Singapore on an aborted three-year Arts scholarship, I had always been cocooned by family and friends in the familiar environs of Seremban. The idea of seeking my fortunes elsewhere had never crossed my mind and now here I was, exiled to Batu Pahat.

My lack of enthusiasm for Batu Pahat was compounded by the fact I was the bearer of bad tidings as well. I'd been asked to deliver a "termination of service" letter from Cathay to the incumbent manager. On the way from Singapore I rehearsed various scenarios of the dreaded moment. The situation was ripe for the sort of bizarre confrontation where I could imagine myself saying, "Hello, I'm Kee Hung. You're fired and I'm your replacement. Close the door when you leave." That was too melodramatic and harsh. Perhaps a gentler approach would be better: "Hello, my name is Kee Hung and I'm really sorry to have to tell you that I've been sent here as your replacement. Take your time packing up your things. Please close the door when you leave, thanks." Or, I could just remain silent and let the poor man read the letter.

Fortunately, the handover did not turn out to be as awkward as I'd feared since the incumbent manager had been forewarned – a piece of information that had been neglected in my briefing. So I finally found myself in charge of the grand sounding Cathay Batu

Pahat, which was actually nothing more than a converted wooden godown with benches, seating about 300 people, filling the space between a white screen in front and the film projector behind. It was probably not too different from the Odeon in Seremban, I thought ruefully, but how was it that my fellow trainee, Lim, was lucky enough to be given charge of the grander 1200-seat Pavilion?

The company didn't provide accommodation so I rented a room in one of the town houses and slept on my foldable camp bed, protected by my mosquito net. Meals were simple affairs taken at the hawker stalls or coffee shops, and a washer woman took care of my laundry. My pay was $200 a month, which was the highest salary I'd ever drawn so far. Half of it was sent back to the family in Seremban and the remaining half was just enough to cover my rental and living expenses, leaving nothing to set aside as savings. I consoled myself that at least I was getting paid regularly and it was a relief to be out of my previous financial quagmire.

Batu Pahat is only about a hundred miles from Seremban but I still felt isolated. I hadn't been with Cathay long enough to accrue any leave to make a quick trip back, so my only recourse was to write home. That wasn't easy either. I didn't have the luxury of being able to compose my thoughts and put pen to paper in the privacy of my rented room given that it was totally devoid of furniture. As a result, my letters were really windows to the stolen moments of reflection in the office where at least I had a desk to write on. It was a bleak period for me. I was homesick. In the spartan confines of my room I would lie on my camp bed and stare at the ceiling, lost in thought. Once, I dreamt that I was cast adrift on a bamboo raft, at the mercy of the currents and foam-flecked eddies of a wide, fast-flowing river. I had no paddle and the only way home was to swim to the distant banks and try to beat a path through the dense, steamy jungle. As I contemplated diving into the moody teal waters, the ruffled waves slapping against my pitiful vessel seemed to speak to me.

When I woke up, I could not remember what was being said for the words had rippled past my consciousness. Although I was at a loss as to the significance of the dream and its oneiric message, it made me wonder whether I had made a mistake by signing up with Cathay. But then, what other choice did I have?

If I was really honest with myself, the chance to determine my own future had slipped through my fingers half a life time before. I had been a sedulous student and from Standard 4 up to Senior Cambridge done well enough to be ranked among the top two of my class every year, generating an intense rivalry with another high-achiever as we both vied for the first or second placing. My strong academic performance earned me a scholarship to Raffles College in Singapore. My parents brimmed with pride for, like most parents, they placed a high value on their children's education, especially when they themselves had had to struggle through life with little or no formal schooling. My father was ecstatic that the scholarship took care of school fees, board and lodging for he still had three other children to support. Everybody expected a promising future ahead of me. Short of an overseas university degree, a college credential was the next best guarantee in opening doors of opportunities.

Unfortunately, sunny days can be ruined by a tropical downpour, and mine was washed away in the second year when I encountered problems with one of the teachers over my "attitude". I've always tried to avoid conflict situations that arise from the bluntness of frank discourse, and would rather feign agreement than face the unpleasant possibility of being exposed to the raw emotions roiling beneath the surface. That didn't necessarily mean that I accepted the other person's viewpoint; I would, for example, surreptitiously carry on doing what I wanted to if I thought I could get away with it. It was what Chen teasingly labelled my "sly stubbornness"—only in this case my behaviour was interpreted as "veiled arrogance" by the teacher. Things just spiralled downhill from there and I ended up failing History in the second-year final exam. My scholarship was on the condition that I pass all the exams every year, and therefore I had no choice but to leave.

Instead of slinking home filled with chagrin, I waltzed back with an air of insouciance that declared to the world that it didn't really matter to me. I reasoned it wasn't my fault, and in many ways was glad to be going home for I missed my friends.

Although I was involved in school sports at the college, I didn't have much of a social life outside, not being able to afford the expense of venturing beyond the school grounds and exploring Singapore aside from organised school excursions. The school and the student quarters became a prison from which I was glad to be released, and this made it easier for me to shrug away the regrettable circumstances of my freedom. I was confident that it would turn out alright somehow and hubris helped me ignore my father's stony displeasure. I could not turn back the clock to undo the past but I could at least try to endure my present tribulations in the hope of a better future: I simply couldn't afford to fail again.

Whilst in Batu Pahat I played tennis at weekends. I had been a keen sportsman during my student days and a member of the school football, hockey and cricket teams. I'd even had a stab at gymnastics and the shot put. I'd enjoyed swimming and made trips to Port Dickson whenever I'd got the chance. Tennis was a game that I picked up only after leaving school and by then I was also involved with the Seremban basketball and volleyball teams where my height was a welcome advantage.

As I settled into a routine in Batu Pahat, I was pleasantly surprised to find some familiar faces from Seremban who were also working in the same town. The branch manager of the Chinese Overseas Bank was a fellow "Paulian" and classmate and the lady who ran the hairdressing saloon was not only from Seremban

Managing the Cathay in Malacca proved to be quite an experience.

but a relative of my good friend, Chen! Living in Chiseled Rock became more tolerable after that.

Cry Me a River

I had hardly warmed my seat as a cinema manager in Batu Pahat when I was told to pack up and head for the historic city of Malacca. Originally a tiny fishing village, it grew to become a major centre for the spice trade but was later overtaken by the other Straits Settlements of Penang and Singapore. Having been variously ruled by the Portuguese, Dutch and then the British, its eclectic heritage imparted a unique flavour to the city.

Cathay planned to open a cinema in Malacca and I wanted to believe that I was being sent there because they had the utmost confidence in me and not because it was acquiring more cinemas than it had seasoned managers to spare. Regardless of the reason, the relocation meant moving half-way closer to Seremban, and that was certainly a pleasing thought.

The cinema, located in Tranquerah Street, had formerly been a stage theatre that belonged to a rich Malaccan businessman. After renovations, it opened in July 1948 as the Cathay Malacca. I stayed in a rented room again. Since it was only about half a mile from my workplace and the landlady was also catering my three daily meals, I arranged for my old New Hudson bicycle to be brought over from Seremban so that I could dash back for lunch and supper.

Managing the Cathay in Malacca proved to be quite an experience. When *Tears of the Yangtze*, a drama about the Japanese occupation of China, was screened, it struck a chord with the public. It was full house for all three daily screenings. Orderly queuing was unknown in those days and the cinema lobby would look like a riot zone, with a frenzied crowd jostling and clambering over each other in their rush to get tickets. The box office itself had a small opening for the transaction of money for tickets but was otherwise protected by wire mesh and iron grills.

The movie was a tear jerker that tugged at the hearts of both

The Cathay Malacca advertising its big hit, Tears of the Yangtze.

men and women in the audience, who left a landslide of tissue paper at the end of every show. The popularity of this poignant tale also spawned black market ticket sales by opportunists looking to make a fast buck. This caught the attention of gangsters and it wasn't too long before I was approached by a gang leader nicknamed "Big Nine" who basically wanted a monopoly on all ticket sales to *Tears of the Yangtze*. Touting was not uncommon in those days, but his demand that tickets be sold exclusively through his gang was clearly unacceptable. With the unspoken threat of unpleasant repercussions if I didn't comply left hanging in the air—my biggest fear was a disruption of cinema operations through vandalism, or violence inflicted on my staff—I had to quickly find a way to resolve the situation. Reporting it to the police wasn't really an option as Malacca was rife with secret societies that stretched the resources of the law and frankly, there was nothing concrete for them to act on at that point. Of course, by the time something "serious" meriting the attention of the police occurred, it would be far too late.

I decided to reason with Big Nine by first pointing out that touting on such a large scale would either provoke a public outcry, forcing the police to be involved, or spark a clash with other gangs jealous of the "easy money" going his way. I put forward my counter proposal that each member of his gang —there were about eight of them—would be allowed to purchase a maximum of five tickets per show. In reality, anyone could buy more than one ticket, although how they used or disposed of them was beyond my control, but by persuading Big Nine to accept the alternative arrangement I was able to maintain a proper tally of legitimate ticket sales, avoid trouble with the underworld and curtail what could have been a nightmare of unrestrained touting. It was my baptism of fire as a cinema manager.

It was in Malacca that I encountered Ah-Yong again.

Ah-Yong had left the soft drinks factory in Seremban probably for the same reasons as me and landed a job as a car salesman in Malacca with Wearne Brothers Motors, the largest automotive company in Malaya at that time. Having just arrived, he had no place to stay and sought me out. I gladly offered to share my room with him as we had got along well as fellow employees at NSAW, but more so because I couldn't very well turn down someone in need of help. Since I only had the one camp bed, Ah-Yong slept on the floor using a mat for bedding. This was a minor inconvenience for someone who used to sleep on the ground in the jungle.

Ah-Yong wasn't his real name, of course, but a sobriquet. His real name was Khoo, a former member and officer of the Malaya People's Anti-Japanese Army (MPAJA) that was the paramilitary wing of the Malayan Communist Party. Most MPAJA members were ethnic Chinese who believed in Communism or were Communist sympathisers. At the same time, there were also those who did not subscribe to the ideology but joined the MPAJA because it represented the only viable local resistance force against the Japanese: Ah-Yong was one such person.

When the war ended, the MPAJA no longer had a raison d'être and was disbanded, its leaders festooned with medals and ribbons from the British government. The Malayan Communist Party itself continued to exist as an organisation in post-war Malaya until the killings of the three plantation managers in the northern Malayan state of Perak by "communist guerrillas" triggered the

Malayan Emergency on 18th June 1948 and the banning of the Party four weeks later.

In the ensuing months it seemed that anyone with the slightest connection to the MCP or the MPAJA was being hunted by the authorities. Across the whole of Malaya, thousands were arrested. Alarmed by this, Khoo was contemplating fleeing into the jungle that had once served as his refuge during the war, only this time he would be hiding from the British. Fortunately, a timely phone call from our ex-boss Yin deflected him from this visceral impulse. Yin was well aware of Khoo's background—in fact, he was the one who filled me in after introducing Khoo to me back at NSAW— and sought to rescue his former employee from dire straits.

A side benefit of running a cabaret that was patronised by senior British officers as well as enlisted men was that it provided Yin with the right contacts to plead for Khoo's freedom. This he did by offering himself as a guarantor, and Yin excitedly informed Khoo that he had obtained an agreement from the authorities. There was one catch though: Khoo had to make his way back to Seremban first, for Yin's pledge as guarantor would only be honoured there. This wasn't going to be an easy task given that Khoo's face was plastered on "wanted" posters everywhere.

Despite the obvious risk of being spotted and arrested, Khoo concluded that being confined in Seremban was preferable to the freedom of the jungle. Bidding me farewell, Khoo took the first available bus out of Malacca, gambling on the fact that most people would fail to make the mental juxtaposition between the ordinary-looking man in civilian clothes and the picture of the gaunt-looking soldier in khaki uniform wearing a cloth cap emblazoned with three red stars. His bold move paid off and he made it to the sanctuary of Seremban without incident.

Although the authorities kept their promise not to jail Khoo, they were still wary and wanted to keep an eye on him. With calculated inspiration, they created a clerical post for Khoo in the Seremban Central Police Station, for what better place to monitor someone than to have him surrounded by policemen? Meanwhile, it was business as usual at the Negri Sembilan Cabaret, and Khoo ended up helping out at the dance hall in the evenings.

I was reasonably happy in Malacca. The cinema was housed in a proper building and not just a converted wooden shed. I had a staff of eighteen people and wasted no time in appointing an assistant manager from amongst them because it seemed like the sensible thing to do. There were no further incidents with the gangsters, partly because the movies that followed did not achieve the same overwhelming success as the *Tears of the Yangtze* and although there were still minor instances of touting, that could not be helped. To top it off, I was able to see my sweetheart, Wei, once again.

I first met her in 1935, the very year that I was getting married and in a further twist of irony, she was teaching in a

Chinese school in Mantin, which was also the hometown of my bride. Mantin was a sleepy little town so Wei spent her weekends in the relatively livelier environ of nearby Seremban, renting a room on Lemon Street next to the Seremban Chinese Recreation Club where I was a member. We were introduced by a mutual acquaintance.

Wei was born in Taiping which is in the state of Perak. Her Hainanese father was formerly a tailor who relocated to Labu, about ten miles east of Seremban, to become a labour supply agent to the rubber plantations; in other words, he provided the "coolies" who tapped the trees for latex. His business prospered to the extent that he eventually became a rubber estate owner himself and could afford to send his young daughter to boarding school in Canton, China. She was lucky to have a father who was progressive in his outlook and did not discriminate between sexes when it came to educational opportunities.

Sadly, her father contracted typhoid and died in a Malaccan hospital whilst she was still studying overseas. Her mother also passed away shortly after, leaving Wei and her younger brother as the two surviving members of the family. Actually, there was an elder sister but she had been given away at birth—Wei's parents at that time were barely able to clothe and feed themselves—and could no longer be traced. Since Wei and her brother were still minors, the estate came under the control of trustees. After completing her studies, Wei returned to Malaya anticipating a comfortable life funded by her inheritance, but this idle dream was shattered when the trustees declared that she and her brother had no legal claim to the estate. They argued that her father had been remiss in drawing up a proper will and therefore their rights as heirs were vitiated. She was shocked by the announcement, confused by the legal technicalities and embittered by the fiduciary betrayal of those who were supposed to look after the family's interests. No longer entitled to an allowance, she was left penniless and bereft of recourse to wrest back what was rightfully theirs.

However, there was something that her father had bequeathed her that nobody could take away: an education. Wei registered herself as a Chinese-language teacher with the Malaya Education Department and thereafter started to earn her own living.

I was sympathetic to Wei's plight and admired her plucky spirit. For someone brought up with servants to attend to every need and later to enjoy the privilege of schooling overseas, it must have been a rude awakening to discover that she now had to work just to survive. When she transferred to a school in Seremban a year later, I persuaded my father to let her stay in one of the spare rooms at our house in Murray Street to save her the trouble of renting a room. Just before the war, her brother died in Malacca. He was only twenty-three and the circumstances of his death were never fully explained to Wei, who was now all alone in the world. During the Occupation she gave private tuition in the day—the Japanese were not as adamant in censuring the teaching of Mandarin—cycling from home to home clad in her *samfoo*, and in the evenings she worked at the same amusement park as I did, albeit at a different stall.

Given our frequent contact and the fact that she was living under the same roof, who can say exactly when our hearts strayed from the shores of friendship to deeper waters? In any case, the events flowing from my decision to join Cathay tested the depth of our relationship when it became apparent that my absence from Seremban could stretch for an indefinite period. I wrote to her regularly during my brief tenure in Batu Pahat. Malacca's proximity to Seremban was a chance perigee of posting that made it a little easier for her to visit me but there was no guarantee of its permanency, and I could be moved out at any time. We discussed our predicament and came to the conclusion that the solution was for Wei to follow me. Wei therefore resigned from her teaching post in Seremban and took up a short-term teaching contract with one of the schools in Malacca. We were reunited at last.

Stand Up and Be Counted

Singapore was not included in the short-lived Malayan Union or the Federation of Malaya that replaced it and remained a crown colony. With its trade, productivity and social services restored to their pre-war levels by 1949, the tiny equatorial island of just under a million people was poised for an economic boom. Other changes were less obvious, involving a subtle shift in perception: although the diverse ethnic communities of Singapore had rejoiced in their liberation from the Japanese and welcomed the return to colonial rule, the spectre of the British defeat by an Asian country had undermined their colonial masters' image of superiority.

Not Just Any Road

Cathay continued to grow and in mid-1949 I was asked to return to Singapore to take charge of two cinemas, the Alhambra and Marlborough, located along Beach Road. Wei had gone into our "arrangement" with her eyes opened and accepted my re-assignment as the nature of my job. The camp bed and mosquito net accompanied me as usual, but I had to return

The Alhambra Cinema, Singapore.

my bicycle to my father's dental clinic at 13 Locke Road in Seremban.

My father, Kok Hing, was already in his seventies and it was actually my sister, Ching, who carried on the business. Ching used to hang around our father watching him work and eventually he allowed her to help him out on simple tasks, fanning her childhood curiosity into a passion that eventually led her to adopt dentistry as a profession. He was pleased to have one of his children follow in his footsteps and took her under his wing as an apprentice. Ching gained a strong empirical grounding under his guidance but although our father was a registered dentist, he had picked up his skills on the job, so Ching went on to acquire the specialised knowledge and techniques of the trade by studying advanced dentistry in Japan. Whilst my father was able to make an adequate living from the dental practice, it was really under Ching's care that the business began to prosper. Her professionalism, coupled with her gentle nature, reassured patients and being the sole female dentist in town gave her a distinct advantage over her competitors since women felt more at ease being attended to by someone of their own gender. Ching remained dedicated to her work and never married, although lingering maternal instincts led her to adopt a baby girl much later in her life.

I don't really know much about my father's past except that he was from the province of Canton in China. I surmised that he spent a number of years in the Portuguese colony of Macau, given that he often spoke wistfully about the place whenever he puffed on his opium pipe, but I have no idea what he was doing there. He migrated to Nanyang (a term used by mainland Chinese to refer to Southeast Asia in general) at the turn of the century when he was in his thirties and made his living as a wandering roadside medicine seller, travelling from town to town, hitching a ride on a bullock cart whenever he could. As a medicine seller he must have been asked for cures for toothaches in the beginning and then later, whether he could remove the rotten teeth as well. I'm sure that's how the extracting of teeth eventually became part of his services.

As a child, I used to hear him boast about how he placated an agitated customer who accused him of pulling out the wrong tooth by offering to extract the correct one for free. I never found out whether he was spinning a yarn or relating a true incident. Having saved up some money, he settled down in Seremban and opened his dental practice, which to me was a daring move, but then again his action typified the dauntless spirit of pioneers of his generation. He was also a self-taught physician who gleaned his knowledge from Chinese medical journals and provided traditional healing services on the sideline as a *sinseh*. If the steady number of patients who came to him was any indication, he was apparently quite good at it, and this provided a welcome source of additional income.

At the age of thirty-six, he must have felt it was time to start a family and brought my mother, Kwai Ho, over from China. She was also from Canton but a different county. Like most of the other poor maidens in her village, she was illiterate but had been taught to cook and do household chores. She bore my father five children but the first, a boy, died soon after birth. I was the second child (and therefore became the eldest) followed by Ching, another sister and a brother.

The family home was also at Locke Road, and in Chinese the name translates to "prostitute lane", apparently in reference to the brothels that used to exist there. It's either an urban myth resulting from the phonetic play on the English word "Locke", or that the vice trade had long vanished from the neighbourhood for I never stumbled across any dens of iniquity that might have led me astray in all the years living in that street. We stayed in a typical terrace house that had a narrow frontage but elongated interior with an air-well in the middle, followed by the kitchen-cum-dining area. At the back, concrete steps led up to the outhouse with its squat toilet and old-fashioned bucket waste-removal system. What should have been the living room at the front had been converted into the dental clinic, whilst sleeping quarters on the upper storey were accessible by a steep flight of wooden stairs.

The dowry from my marriage that I mentioned earlier enabled my father to relocate members of the family to a rented house at 96 Murray Street (except for Ching who remained at Locke Road with our parents to look after the business). It was also to be my new home as a married man. I was quite sad to leave, even though it meant having more elbow room and privacy at Murray Street. I have a strong sentimental attachment to the house at Locke Road for it was not only where I grew up, but also where I was born as my mother gave birth to all of us, with the aid of midwives, at home and not in a hospital.

It was quite a common practice in those days. It was also quite common for parents in such cases to be a bit tardy in registering births; hence the recorded date of 14th September on my birth certificate is not the actual day I was born. It is, in fact, a few months earlier on the 25th day of the 6th moon of the Year of the

Pig. I never bothered to check for the Gregorian equivalent[2] to mark my birthday as that date would shift each year for nineteen years before the Chinese and Gregorian calendars synchronised and threw up the same date again. It was easier to mark my birthday according to the lunar calendar.

Demand for Attention

I didn't have to ferret out my own accommodation in Singapore as there was an empty room upstairs at the rear of the Alhambra that I could make use of. It even had an adjacent shower and toilet. Some old, unwanted chairs lying about the cinema suddenly found new lease of life as furniture in my bedroom. It was certainly an improvement from my previous rented accommodations. As for Wei, she would come to Singapore as soon as she'd completed her contract with the school in Malacca.

The Alhambra had undergone minor renovations and was re-opened in July with the screening of *Casbah*, a musical remake of the film *Algiers*. The cinema showed mostly English films. Serials like *Dick Tracy*, *Fu Manchu*, *Flash Gordon* and *Undersea Kingdom* were immensely popular. Such serials were made up of episodes lasting about twenty minutes or so, and when all the episodes were strung together it could extend the length of the show to over three hours, making it necessary for me to reduce

---

[2] 20th July

daily screenings from four to three. Ardent fans could be thrilled by the exploits of their heroes unfolding seamlessly in cool air-conditioned comfort, which was in stark contrast to when I was first introduced to the world of cinemas in my early teens back in Seremban. Those were the pioneer days of the roving film exhibitors and makeshift cinemas.

On a tract of land at the end of Jalan Tunku Hassan, there used to be a large tent with benches occupying up to half the space inside, whilst the other half was strewn with wooden planks. There was a small piano at one end and the screen hung six to eight feet above it. Ten cents bought you space on the bench and five cents got you a stiff neck sitting in front on the planks. There was only one show a day and it was held after sunset since the tent's material was not thick enough to stop the fading glory of the setting sun from suffusing the interior with its dying light. Fifteen minutes before the beginning of a show, a pianist would provide musical entertainment to a restless audience who would whistle, clap and shout in joyful relief when the lights dimmed as it signalled the end of their wait.

The operator of the single projector had to crank a handle to get the film rolling, and it was quite amusing to see the flickering images on the screen sometimes jump about frenetically and at other times move at a sluggish pace. It all depended on the projectionist being able to maintain a constant speed in turning the handle, but being human he couldn't help but wax and wane according to whether he was experiencing an adrenaline burst or was feeling tired and morose. This was still the period of silent films and a sound effects man sat behind the screen equipped with an empty kerosene tin and a stick. He was especially busy when cowboy movies were shown because every time the images showed a gun being fired, he had to beat the kerosene tin with his stick. Sometimes he was inattentive and missed his cue, and such lapses would draw shouts of derision from the audience.

The shows lasted an hour and a quarter and typically opened with a newsreel, followed by a short comedy and then four reels (equivalent to two episodes) of a serial. When a reel of film ended, the lights would come on and there would be a short break as there was only the one projector and the reels had to be changed. The number of episodes for different serials varied, but with each episode ending in a cliffhanger, patrons had to keep coming back to find out what happened next. As I did not have enough pocket money, I resorted to slipping under the tent after the lights were turned off and the show had started. I wasn't always successful though, as a watchman patrolled the perimeter with a cane. Still, I managed to catch most of the twenty episodes of *Perils of Pauline* as well as *Tarzan of the Apes*.

Next door to the Alhambra was the smaller Marlborough that also underwent renovation and re-opened a few months later. It screened mainly Indian and Chinese films but the audience here had to be content with ceiling fans, one of which actually dropped off, fortunately not during a show so no one was hurt. It was more likely that someone would be injured from an unruly mob of ticket buyers pushing and elbowing each other to get to the front—a situation reminiscent of my experience at Cathay Malacca. We had our two Sikh watchmen deployed to keep the crowd under control, but they were ineffectual and I couldn't really fault them for there was little that they could do when what was required was a riot squad. Next to the Marlborough, there was a side road leading to the seafront and where Tay Koh Yat buses were often parked. In the evening, Malay hawkers would set up their satay stalls. Hunched over their portable stoves, they would fan the charcoal fires, impregnating the night with the tantalizing smoky smell of skewered grilled meats that drew throngs of customers who sat huddled around makeshift tables as they feasted under the stars.

I was fast learning that managing a cinema involved more than what I'd been taught as a trainee. A great deal had to be picked up on the job. One of the lessons—unwritten rule No 1—was to always appoint an assistant manager to help share the load. I'd done this in Malacca and now with two cinemas to look after it was crucial to have an assistant. The person I selected for the post was Lau, who was to play an important role in my life a year and a half later.

Another lesson—unwritten rule No 2—was to retain a calm

presence of mind when handling sensitive situations, particularly when it involved a jingoistic journalist. The re-establishment of Singapore as a British crown colony meant a return to the practice of playing the British national anthem in cinemas at the end of each show. The audience had to stand to attention until the last refrain of "God Save the King" (in this case the royal personage was King George VI, who ruled from 1936 to 1952). Only then could the cinema patrons leave. However, it was mainly Englishmen who observed this protocol and the rest of the audience—of mixed ethnic origins and nationalities—were anxious to scoot off earlier. To avoid a crush of people and possible injury, the staff manning the doors opened them even before the anthem had ended.

Riled by this practise, a young English reporter came to see me. He argued that the premature opening of the exit doors was disrespectful to the King of England and demanded that I tell my employees to desist from such action. I tried to soothe him by calmly explaining that the door-keepers were merely ensuring the safety of the cinemagoers by allowing egress to those who wanted to leave earlier, otherwise the exits would be impossibly jammed with people. Disgruntled with what he perceived was an unsatisfactory and unpatriotic response, the brash young man made public his complaint in an article in the following day's local newspaper. This resulted in a phone call from the general manager, Ede (the very same person that I had approached for a job in Seremban two years before). Ede had spluttered when he'd spotted the article in the morning newspaper and, upset by the unflattering portrayal of Cathay, he pressed me for an explanation. I told him dispassionately what had happened. After listening to my side of the story, Ede was satisfied that the Cathay staff had acted in the public's interest, with no intention of deliberately affronting the Crown, and considered the matter a "storm in a tea cup".

Nevertheless, I felt compelled by a sense of discretion to instruct the door-keepers that, in future, they should only lift up the locking bars but not open the doors. Those patrons who wanted to leave early could do so of their accord by just nudging the doors open.

Intermission

Although leaving Seremban had opened the gateway to a new life, it separated me from my children. My wife and I tried not to let our own personal resentments spill over to our offspring, so we bestowed upon them the affection that was missing in our relationship. Being away from Seremban meant I spent even less time with the children than usual. My son, Casey, was already thirteen years old and enrolled in my old school, St Paul's, whilst my eleven-year-old daughter Yiwa was studying at St Francis Convent. I felt a sense of guilt for having neglected the kids and suggested that perhaps the two of them might come and stay with me during their school break.

It was their first visit to a big city and both were visibly excited and, I guessed, also slightly apprehensive about spending time with a father whom they had seen very little of for one and a half years. Memory behaves in strange ways and takes many forms. Sometimes it is a sieve that strains all features of an event, leaving only a vague misshapen fact of the occasion itself ... and that too might dissolve in time. Sometimes it is a hidden oubliette in the deepest recess of your mind, holding prisoner every detail of the past until released by some key, such as a picture, a smell, a sound, or in the case of my son, by stepping inside a cinema.

After picking up the two kids from the station, I took them to Alhambra and was showing them around when Casey spontaneously blurted out his recollection of having accompanied me and Wei to a movie in Seremban. He could even name the film and the movie stars. By that time, Seremban had, of course, acquired cinemas of a more permanent nature. The Sapphire had replaced the "tent cinema" at Jalan Tunku Hassan—the piano now relocated to the foot of the proscenium – and carried on the tradition of screening silent, black-and-white serials but included more comedies, like the *Keystone Cops* and the classics of Charlie Chaplin. The first so-called "talkie" shown at the Sapphire was *Wings*, a movie about World War I fighter pilots. It was technically still a silent movie as the only sounds were of aeroplane engines that were reproduced from a gramophone player synchronised with the film. It was a bit of a letdown but the aerial combat scenes were spectacular.

When the first true talkie—I think it was a musical called *Sunny Side Up*—was shown, it seemed like magic. I still remember the title of one of the songs: "If I had a Talking Picture of You".

When a second cinema, the Plaza, came up we were spoilt for choice. Coming back to the occasion that Casey mentioned, the film in question was *Bathing Beauty*, a light-hearted romantic comedy starring Red Skelton and Esther Williams, and my son was the ten-year-old chaperone on one of my outings with Wei. She loved the film and though my taste in movies leaned towards the "action" genre, I took pleasure in the fact that she enjoyed it. I told my kids that, if they liked, they could watch movies at the Alhambra. They beamed with anticipation.

Wasting no time, the three of us engaged in a host of activities over the next couple of days: we went out for a sampan boat ride at the seafront near Beach Road; swam at the Chinese Swimming Club where I was a member and made a trip to the Tiger Balm Gardens Chinese theme park to gawk at the graphic depiction of excruciating tortures, customised according to the sin committed, meted out in the Ten Courts of Hell. There was an aeroplane exhibition being held at Kallang Airport, so we went along to have a peek, hoping to spot the five-seater Air Speed Consul that Malayan Airways used for its inaugural commercial flight from Singapore to Kuala Lumpur. However, what impressed us was the large and spacious twenty-two-seater DC3 that was rumoured to offer the luxury of in-flight service. And, of course, I brought them to the satay stalls next to the Marlborough.

All too soon it was time for Casey and Yiwa to return home, and whilst they had thoroughly enjoyed themselves, especially watching movies in the cinema, I think they were also relieved that they didn't have to sleep in my room anymore. Access to my bedroom was up the stairs via the backstage. It didn't help matters that in entertaining them with whimsical accounts of my experiences in Malacca, I had rattled off the story of the obdurate night watchman who'd resisted my attempts to get him to sleep inside the cinema because he believed in the rumours that the Cathay Malacca was haunted! The telling of this tale had the unfortunate effect of spooking the kids, and their imaginations ran wild each time they had to brave the fuliginous gloom and eerie silence of the empty cinema hall.

It seemed that I was never to stay in one place for long. By the latter half of 1949 Cathay, through acquisitions or partnerships, had a chain of theatres across Malaya from Penang down to Singapore. But Dato Loke was relentless in looking for new expansion opportunities and this came in the form of a proposed partnership in Kuching. The owners of two cinemas over there wanted Cathay's involvement, specifically to supply English films. Dato Loke agreed but on the condition that the theatres be managed by Cathay. And so the instruction went out to find someone willing to shoulder the responsibility of being the sole Cathay representative, in a distant land, isolated from headquarters—and I was approached.

Having been with Cathay for almost two years now, I wanted to believe that they'd picked me because my talents had been recognised and not because everyone else they'd spoken to had cringed at the thought of being exiled to a rustic and remote location, instantly proffering a litany of reasons as to why they couldn't go. To tell the truth, part of me wasn't keen to leave either. The reason had nothing to do with any anticipated hardships but the fact that Wei had just moved to Singapore a few months before. She was staying with her friends in Katong, on the east coast, and had been fortunate enough to land a teaching job at a rural school in Tampines, which proved fortuitous as it was also located in the east. Having just transplanted herself to Singapore in order to join me, she reacted with consternation to the news that the company now wanted to send me overseas.

Although Sarawak was a crown colony like Singapore, it was not conveniently located next door but was five hundred miles across the South China Sea. For all intents and purposes, it was a foreign country: an applicant looking for a job in Sarawak was subjected to a lengthy bureaucratic process of obtaining the necessary documents and for a single woman with no local friends to stand as guarantor for her, it was an uphill task. Even if she could overcome all the obstacles, my itinerant job could well have me careening to some other unexpected destination by the time she set foot in Kuching. All these considerations brought home the uncertainties of her nomadic existence that had seemed so wonderfully romantic when she'd first embarked on it but was now causing her distress and placing me in a dilemma.

Although I was told that I would receive a salary adjustment— from $280 that I was earning to $375—and was given the assurance that my accommodation would be taken care of by the local partners, these inducements had no bearing on my decision of whether to accept the assignment or not. I wish that I could say that I was gripped by a lust for adventure, eager to leap into the unknown. After all, my whirlwind tour of duty in different locations had opened my eyes to new horizons and I no longer clung to the parochial view that Seremban was the centre of the world. Or that my conscience was pricking me, reminding me that I still needed to prove to my friend Ng that his unconditional faith in me had not been misplaced. However, my motivations were more prosaic. I was still a relatively "new" employee and I didn't think that my "bosses" would take kindly to me declining the transfer; I did not wish to bear the stigma of being a recalcitrant employee who was fussy about his postings. Also, for the first time in my working life I was holding a decent job with a modest but still agreeable remuneration that freed me from the tribulation of always teetering on the edge of subsistence: I didn't want to jeopardise what I had gained. My wish to become a cinema manager had been realised and if the currents that dictated my direction seemed baffling, they were also benign if my progress so far was any indicator. Having made up my mind, I promised Wei that I would return for her as soon as possible. She accepted my words with mixed feelings but agreed to stay and wait for me in Singapore.

Kuching is the capital of Sarawak which is on the island of Borneo. That was about the extent of my knowledge and whether it reflected a general misconception or it was my reluctance to leave Wei, I made the mistake of asking for an entry visa to North Borneo—a separate British crown colony also in Borneo—instead of Sarawak. In any case, the error was discovered and rectified in time and I was ready to sail to an unfamiliar shore.

Episode 4

Pepper Barons and Jokers Wild

Sarawak was the southernmost province of the Sultanate of Brunei, but by the 19th century the Sultanate's hold over this area had weakened to the extent that it was infested with pirates and wracked by rebellion. When the English adventurer James Brooke sailed into Kuching in 1839 on his well-armed schooner, the Royalist, *the Sultanate took the opportunity to enlist his aid to restore peace to the region. In return, James Brooke was rewarded with a piece of territory and installed as the Rajah of Sarawak in 1842. Thus began the dynasty of the White Rajahs that lasted for a century.*

After the Second World War, the third Rajah Brooke, Vyner Brooke, who had taken refuge in Sydney during the war years, felt that the future of Sarawak was safer with Britain and had the local state council put it to a vote. For three days the council agonised over the issue before agreeing by a narrow margin of nineteen votes against sixteen, reflecting the divided feelings of the populace. On 1st July 1946, Sarawak became a British colony.

Cat City

On Friday, 28th October 1949 I boarded the steamer, aptly named the *Rajah Brooke*, for Kuching. This was a newly built ship, the second to bear the name as the original had been lost in 1896. It had an enlarged carrying capacity of two hundred deck passengers and twenty-two first-class passengers, whose company I didn't have the privilege of enjoying since I belonged to the former category. Although commercial air services to Borneo had recently been established, the journey by sea was still the main (and cheaper) mode of travel to Kuching.

Stuck on a boat plying the South China Sea, there was little else to do except reflect on the events that had catapulted me to this moment and ponder on what lay ahead. Such idyllic

Preparing for departure at Clifford Pier, Singapore.

contemplation never materialised for I was distracted by the queasy, churning feeling in my stomach induced by the undulating waves. The pallor of my face must have cycled through various shades of chartreuse as I hung my head over the railing.

This wasn't the first time I had travelled on a boat. When I was about five or six years old, my parents made a trip back to China with me in tow and my sister Ching, who was barely two years old, strapped to my mother's back in a cloth cradle. We had to make our way to Singapore first and then board a crowded *tongkang* (bumboat) that ferried us to a steamer bound for Hong Kong. Seated at the bottom of the *tongkang* and surrounded by adults, all I could see was the sky above, just like the proverbial frog at the bottom of the well. I don't remember much about the actual journey to Hong Kong or how we got to the mainland after that.

Being so young at that time, I have only disjointed memories of our sojourn in China. If it was my mother's intention to return to her distant village, it was thwarted by rampant rumours of bandits abducting people for ransom, especially those who had returned from overseas as they were thought to be rich and were highly prized as hostages. We stayed with my father's elder brother, who was a devout Catholic, in a small village located on the outskirts of the Kong Moon town. The village comprised twenty brick houses facing each other in two rows of ten, separated by a narrow lane. My cousins and I were running about playing in that lane when I accidentally trampled on a duckling. It wasn't my fault but my mother gave me a thrashing anyway.

I got into trouble again when I joined my cousins in their mischievous crusade of smashing joss-stick urns placed at the front door of neighbouring houses. That earned me another beating from my mother, whom you may have guessed was the martinet in the family.

Not all my recollections were made vivid by association with painful punishment; there are also the imprints of poignant moments. Like the time my mother and I walked to the nearby town of Kong Moon. We passed the town jail and I caught sight of a young woman, with a baby strapped to her back, gripping the iron bars tightly with both hands as she tearfully looking out of her cell window. I asked my mother why the woman was locked up—she didn't look like a criminal to me. My mother hazarded a guess that the poor girl had most likely been caught trying to smuggle salt. I didn't understand why smuggling salt was such a wicked act that deserved imprisonment, and felt sorry for the young mother whose plaintive sobs continued to haunt me even after we left Kong Moon.

Again, I don't remember much about our return journey except for the humiliating experience when we disembarked in Singapore. Deck passengers were herded like animals into the bumboats and dumped at St John's Island, which had a lazaretto and was used as a quarantine station to deal with cholera-infected immigrants. We were forced to cleanse ourselves by taking sulphur baths and have all our belongings fumigated before being allowed to step ashore on the main island. When I think about it, the amazing thing about the whole trip was that I was perfectly alright during the long sea voyage to and fro. How I wish I was that innocent child again, granted immunity from motion sickness through sheer ignorance and curious fascination with the game of trying to balance on a rolling deck.

My wretched condition lasted the entire journey of what seemed like an interminable three days, so it was with immense relief that I finally stepped off the boat at Kuching onto solid ground

I stayed in one of these shophouses along the Kuching waterfront.

again. I was met by one of the four local partners and was grateful that the first order of business was to get me settled in. Formal introduction to the staff would take place the next day. We walked to a row of shop houses in the main bazaar next to the waterfront and, anticipating a good rest after my maritime ordeal, I was left speechless when he showed me where I was supposed to stay. My "pre-arranged accommodation" was an upstairs storeroom stacked with baskets bulging with glass and earthenware. Some of them must have been lying there for ages for they were covered with cobwebs. Seeing my look of surprise, my contact offered the deft explanation that the place had been chosen for my convenience since one of the cinemas in my charge was located nearby. I had a flicker of suspicion that the selection of my living quarters had more to do with the local partner's simmering resentment of having to relinquish the actual management of the cinemas to me but I kept my peace, thankful that I would at least be sleeping on a stable floor instead of a ship's deck.

The bathing and toilet facilities were located on the ground floor, in a small courtyard at the back of the building. Taking a bath meant having to douse myself with icy cold water scooped up from a large open tub, and was perforce a hasty affair rather than a leisurely ablution. The toilet utilised buckets like the one in our home at Locke Road and having grown up with this system, I was inured to its malodorous assault, although I know that people have been driven to light up a cigarette to counter the pungent

My "pre-arranged" accommodation.

reek of accumulated human excreta.

However, it was the narrowness of the outhouse that was most vexing and, as I am of fairly large build, it was a test of my adroitness in manoeuvring within the confining walls that were oddly stained with grimy brown streaks. When I learnt of the odious origin of the defacements later, I was even more at pains to avoid brushing against the toilet walls. Let me tell you that I am no stranger to hardship: as a young boy, I had to trudge to school barefooted because my parents couldn't afford to buy me shoes, and at night I had to study by the light of a kerosene lamp because we had no electricity. So even though I had to live in squalid living conditions, I stoically endured them ... at least for the time being.

I was introduced to the staff the next day as planned and among the people I met were Hong the office clerk, Nam the service engineer and Ah-Lee the ticket collector.

As I set about familiarising myself with the place and its people, I noted that the kampongs around town still displayed placards calling for the return of the Rajah. Despite the fact that three years had passed since Sarawak had ceded to Britain, there was still a nostalgic yearning for the golden age of the White Rajahs. Such depth of feeling seemed quaint to me but there was a darker undercurrent. Vyner Brooke, the last Rajah, had promised to move Sarawak towards eventual self-rule by its people, but the war had interrupted the process and post-war developments not only obliterated any prospect of self-government, but Sarawak's very independence when the country was steered into the arms of the British Empire by Vyner Brooke himself. The anti-cessionists refused to give up and continued to campaign actively for a return to their former independent status.

Disenchanted with the lack of progress, a radical splinter group called Rukun Tiga-belas, or Rukun 13, decided to turn from the movement's vociferous but largely peaceful protests to something that could not be ignored: assassination. They chose a highly prominent government figure as their target: the recently installed second British Governor of Sarawak, Duncan Stewart.

On a visit to Sibu as part of his state-wide familiarisation tour, he was stabbed in the abdomen in front of a large crowd. Because of the severity of his wound, he was transferred to a Singapore hospital but he never recovered and died a week later. This incident occurred in December, just a month after my arrival, and was front-page news in Kuching. I was worried that unrest would follow, but whilst the anti-cession supporters were passionate about their cause, many were equally horrified by the killing of the governor. Swift punishment of the perpetrators coupled with a government crackdown on the anti-cession movement served to turn a highly explosive situation into a damp squib. Shortly after, the colonial office appointed Anthony Abell to take over as governor.

The two cinemas that I managed were the Sylvia and the Lilian. The Sylvia was previously owned by the last Rajah, Vyner Brooke, and was named after his wife. When Sarawak was ceded to the British Government, Vyner Brooke sold the Sylvia to the owners of the Lilian. Housed in a single-storey concrete building, the Sylvia had a seating capacity of 450 with chairs that were fixed to the floor. Two specially constructed throne-like chairs still dominated the back, legacies of an era passed when they were used by the Rajah and Ranee on the occasions they dropped by to watch a show. In comparison, the Lilian was much larger with a seating capacity of 750, but it used movable wooden benches

The Sylvia Cinema, Kuching.

with armrests delineating the individual seats. It was originally a theatre with a stage and could put on "live" shows. Neither cinema had numbers affixed to the seats.

One of my first tasks was to resolve the mystery of why both cinemas could at times be packed, with no standing room whatsoever, but actual ticket sales did not match the head count. Prices of tickets then were $1.20, $0.80 and $0.40 for Reserved, 1st Class and 2nd Class respectively. I queried the ticket collectors and learnt that there were many people who unashamedly barged their way in, becoming aggressive if anyone tried to stop them. The matter had been brought to the attention of the previous manager but evinced little sympathy and no support, so the hapless ticket collectors decided to let things be. I addressed the problem by implementing a numbering system where each ticket sold would bear a number corresponding to a specific seat. In addition, I instructed the ticket collectors to be more stringent and promised to back them up by calling the police if necessary. It wasn't easy.

What we take for granted now as normal cinema rules was revolutionary back then in Kuching, and it took at least several months before cinemagoers got used to the idea of assigned seating and the ticket collectors felt empowered to bar those without tickets from entering, especially when they had to deal with the voluble protests of fishermen's wives who had the habit of trooping into the cinema with their brood of half a dozen kids with only one ticket in hand. To help cope with the running of two cinemas, I applied unwritten rule No 1 and made Hong the assistant manager of the Lilian.

Sarawak is known for its pepper which is largely exported. Traditionally, up to eighty percent of the crop is processed into black pepper with the remainder being turned into white pepper. I thought the capital should have been named Pepper City instead of Kuching, which means 'cat' in the Malay language. There are various stories of how the city got its name. One version states that it comes from the Chinese word *ku ching*, which means "old well"; a big well used to exist near the bazaar and Chinese settlements, and was a landmark and reference point for that section of town. Another story claims that the name was taken from the cat's-eye fruit, or *mata kuching*, that grew in abundance in the area. I personally prefer the apocryphal tale of James Brooke's first trip up the river in 1839. As they neared their destination, Brooke asked the native pilot for the name of the village they were approaching. Thinking that he was pointing to the wild feline scampering along the river banks, the local guide replied *"Kucing*!*"*

There were many pepper plantations just a few miles out of Kuching, mainly owned by the Chinese. The two largest dialect groups were the Hakka and the Foochow, who made up about sixty percent of the Chinese population in Sarawak. When Charles Brooke, the nephew of James Brooke, became the second White Rajah in 1868, he encouraged Chinese immigration into Sarawak so that they could help boost the economy. The Hakkas settled in the Kuching and Samarahan divisions of Sarawak and were mainly involved in growing gambier, pepper and other cash crops. The Foochows arrived en masse later with the first big migration in 1901 when they were brought in to help open up the Rejang area through rice farming. But the traditional farming methods that they used successfully back in China were foiled by the different climatic and soil conditions, so they turned to cash crops and eventually concentrated on growing rubber and pepper instead.

Each plantation could harvest on average thirty to forty piculs that fetched the price of $1000 per picul in Kuching at that time (a picul being equivalent to sixty kilograms in the metric system).

That meant each plantation owner collected $30,000–$40,000 cash. Since they didn't trust the banks and stuffing such a large amount under the mattress was not a good idea, they invested in houses instead. Of course, these pepper barons paid for everything in cash.

One such pepper baron insisted on buying tickets to a show even though it was full house. When informed that there were no tickets left for sale, he shouted angrily at the ticket sales girl and dramatically threw down a large bundle of banknotes on the box-office counter. "Is my money no good?" The flustered sales girl didn't know how to deal with such obnoxious behaviour. I was doing my rounds and observed the whole thing so I quickly stepped in.

"Of course your money is good. We don't have any seats but we can sell you as many tickets as you like." Then, with a wicked smile, I pretended to reach for the entire pile of banknotes that, at a guess, must have amounted to several hundred dollars. Taken aback, the pepper baron snatched away his bundle of cash and walked off in a huff. This gave rise to unwritten No 3—which is to confront bluster and bluff with an even bigger bluff but smile when you do so because it looks like you really mean it!

Club Chums

I joined the Kuching Recreation Club where I played tennis for exercise and mahjong to socialise. One of my tennis partners was a local businessman who ran a supermarket in Carpenter Street, catering to expatriates. He also owned a couple of houses, and upon learning of the deplorable living conditions I had to put up with, offered to rent me a room in one of his bungalows. I jumped at the chance to extricate myself from my warehouse woes. The house at Reservoir Road was a raised wooden bungalow with steps leading up to the upper area containing a living room, two bedrooms (one of which I was renting) and a kitchen. The ground level was fenced in by wooden partitions and served as a storage area. And it was still within walking distance to the cinemas.

Some of Kuching's more colourful personalities could be found gathered at the club's mahjong tables; among them was old man Yap, a sprightly gentleman in his seventies who'd sired sixteen children—although it must be said that greater admiration should go to his wife for bearing and raising all his kids but then such was the male chauvinistic stripes of the club. The testosterone-charged Ah-Yap still insisted on driving to the club by himself despite numerous objections from his children. And who could fail to notice the obese, chain-smoking Ah-Puay. With his double chin merging with his thick neck, the rotund civil servant had difficulty in swivelling his head and had to shift his entire body to look behind him, a manoeuvre he carried out one day whilst preparing to reverse his car from the club grounds. Seeing that it was clear, he rotated his bulky torso to face front, and foregoing any further checks that involved turning his head, engaged the reverse gear and backed squarely into a car that had just pulled up. Although the damage was minor, the incident became a major joke that was loudly repeated whenever they saw Ah-Puay about to leave the club. Ah-Puay worked for the Treasury and I used to visit his office every week to pay the cinema entertainment tax. There was a Chartered bank across the street and occasionally I spotted Ah-Puay heading towards it accompanied by an office boy carrying a tray piled high with banknotes. "Aren't you afraid of being robbed?" I asked naively.

"I've been doing this since the Rajah's time," Ah-Puay replied with equanimity. Those were simpler days.

Annual Kuching Regatta by the waterfront.

Hat Trick

The annual Kuching Regatta is a popular event that provides a thrilling spectacle of sleek racing boats surging down the river propelled by the banks of rowers paddling with a furious hypnotic rhythm. The regatta dates back as far as 1872, and historically drew numerous entries from the various ethnic groups, which added colour and diversity in the form of the different designs and styles of boats that were fielded. There was the traditional racing boat of the Melanau called the *bidar*; the Orang Ulus had their "flying boat" with its hornbill bow; the Bidayuh used the *arud* which was normally used for transportation but adapted for the regatta; the Ibans also adapted their *perahu bidar* for competitive river sports and, of course, the unmistakable Chinese dragon boat. These days the competition is no longer confined to locals but involves participants from other countries.

Originally held at the beginning of the year, it was later pushed back to September. I had arrived in Kuching too late to catch the event and had to wait till the following year before I could watch it. The competing boats would travel along the section of the river that wound past the town so spectators usually lined the banks or crowded at the pier. However, my Kuching friends had hired a sampan boat in order to get closer to the action and invited me to join them. It was an excellent opportunity for a ringside view, so I jauntily put on a black fedora which I had taken to wearing when outdoors—both for protection from the sun and for its rakish effect—and went along. As we waited expectantly for the race to start, a sudden gust of wind whipped away my hat, depositing it in the river just next to the sampan. I leaned out to hastily retrieve my prized possession before the current could steal it away and promptly lost my balance, joining my hat with a loud splash. As I was fished out of the river, totally drenched and sheepishly clinging to my limp and sodden fedora, my ears burned at the sound of the unrestrained laughter of my companions. It was amazing how fast the news circulated back to the club.

White Knight and Card Kings

The Malayan "Emergency" was a euphemism for a conflict that could not officially be termed a "war" for the simple reason that insurance coverage was only valid for losses due to riots and civil commotion. Such expediency of labelling tended to misrepresent the situation abroad even as the authorities on the ground struggled to counter the insurgency, and it was only in 1950 that more effective initiatives were implemented.

One such initiative was the resettlement of hundreds of thousands of rural Chinese squatters to fortified villages where they were provided with better living standards and a stake in owning the land, thereby removing them from Communist influence.

As a result, the Communists appeared to lose their momentum but they were far from emasculated: in October 1951, they struck a major blow when they ambushed and killed the British High Commissioner as he was on his way to Fraser's Hill for the weekend. His replacement, General Sir Gerald Templer, arrived in February 1952 with a mandate that granted him full control over the police, military and civil authorities. This heralded a significant policy shift. It still could not be called a war, but the British now fully recognised that they were fighting one.

Rescue

The previous year had been a struggle for me and just when I thought I could relax, the general manager, Ede, decided to undertake an extensive tour of North Borneo and Brunei. It was to be a similar exercise to the one that had sent him all over Malaya three years before—looking at expansion opportunities for Cathay. He made a preliminary stop in Kuching and pulled me and Nam, our service engineer, along. Nam's role was to cast a critical eye over the

On the road visiting outlying cinemas.

condition of the film projectors in the small independent cinema halls that might be potentially acquired by Cathay. The three of us spent two mad, hectic weeks in late October criss-crossing the country by plane, car and train—visiting the island of Labuan, the various towns in Brunei, Sandakan on the east coast of North Borneo and Jesselton on the west coast before Ede decided that he had covered sufficient ground and returned to Singapore. I was really looking forward to taking my annual leave and having a break in Singapore after that exhausting excursion. There was another reason for wanting to go back; I had made a promise to Wei and I intended to keep that promise. But first, there was another matter to attend to.

Not too long before, I'd received a letter from Khoo, who was still in Seremban, asking for my help. He was in trouble again, this time with the Communists who had branded him a "running dog" of the British when they'd found out he was working for the authorities at the police station. Khoo claimed that the Communists had bungled an attempt on his life at the Negri Sembilan Cabaret. A grenade had been lobbed into the crowded dance hall one evening and it was a miracle that no one had been killed in the explosion, although many had been injured. Whether Khoo had been the intended target or the grenade had been meant for the British servicemen who frequented the place was a moot point. Suffice to say, the incident rattled Khoo, who was convinced that he was a marked man. Having once been on the British "wanted" list, he had the dubious honour of now being on the Communist "death" list.

Friendship has always played a major part in my life and it was without hesitation that I offered Khoo the job of assistant manager of the Sylvia, a position that was still vacant. I also undertook to act as his sponsor in Sarawak and submitted all the necessary documents. But the latter's past did not escape the vigilance of the Kuching Immigration Department, and I was summoned to the office of the Chief Immigration Officer where I was asked to explain why I was sponsoring a "known communist".

The chief was an Englishman and he and I happened to be socially acquainted—after all, Kuching was not a very big place—and therefore I knew something of his background. He was not only a war veteran but also one of the lucky survivors of the infamous Burma–Thailand death railway that the Japanese constructed using conscripted Asian labourers and prisoners of war. I probably used the same argument that Yin had when he'd negotiated on Khoo's behalf with the BMA, namely that it was unreasonable to stigmatise Khoo as a communist for opposing the Japanese in the only way he could: and that was to fight for the MPAJA. For good measure I emphasised that Khoo had a lot in common with the chief—they had both bravely fought against the Japanese. I'm not sure whether the chief was swayed by my reasoning or because I, as a respectable member of the business community, was willing to stick my neck out to sponsor someone with past links to the Communists, but approval for Khoo's entry visa was eventually given.

Reunion

With passage booked on the *Rajah Brooke,* I left Kuching on Saturday, 2nd December 1950. I tried to take as few days of my precious annual leave as possible by using the weekends to my advantage. The ship did not get to Singapore till Tuesday and I was wracked by seasickness again for the entire trip but endured it by focusing on the goal ahead. I had finally proposed marriage to Wei.

The law (at that time) did not require customary marriages to be registered for them to be recognised, but by the same token, the abrogation of such marriages had to follow certain separation rites. These could be, for example, the placement of posters around Seremban or an advertisement in the newspaper announcing the intention to nullify a marriage. It was a sort of do-it-yourself decree nisi absolute. None of which were carried out. I was convinced that my extended absence and deliberate avoidance of contact with my first wife was sufficient proof of my intention to sever conjugal ties, and that after three years of separation I was now freed from my traditional marriage vows. I could have married Wei earlier because it wasn't illegal to have more than one wife in those days, but I needed to find my own two feet first and more importantly, I felt that our marriage should start on a clean slate without complications to our relationship. That aside, I felt that now was the right time as I could bring Wei over to Sarawak officially as my wife.

The wedding arrangements had to be carefully planned beforehand for, as I mentioned, I was back for only a week, but that didn't stop Wei from fussing and making last-minute adjustments to the preparations. Three days after my arrival, on Friday, 8th December, we exchanged our marriage vows in a simple ceremony at the Singapore Marriage Registry. It was solemnised by F.M. Grosse and witnessed by Wei's best friend from her Canton school days and Lau, my former assistant manager who was now the current manager of Alhambra.

After that we adjourned to Raffles Photographers studio in Bras Basah Road to have our wedding portraits taken; Wei looked resplendent in her open-necked, flowing wedding gown matched with a cathedral veil and white gloves whilst I was the gallant groom in my new, specially tailored white suit. The following night, we hosted a dinner for a small circle of friends and colleagues at a Cantonese restaurant, renowned for its suckling pigs and shark's fin soup and a popular venue for wedding banquets.

None of my family members from Seremban were present. Aside from the obvious travel inconvenience for my elderly parents, there was also the awkwardness of the situation given that my "ex-wife" was still staying at Murray Street. It seemed best that my marriage to Wei be presented to my family as a fait accompli. The remaining two days were supposed to be devoted to last-minute shopping, which we did on Sunday, but Monday was mostly spent glued to the radio as riots had broken out in parts of Singapore, with acts of violence directed mainly at Europeans and Eurasians. It was sparked by anger over the outcome of a custody battle over a thirteen-year-old girl between her biological Dutch/Eurasian parents and her Malay adoptive parents with the court ruling in favour of the former.

The situation remained tense on the day we boarded the *Rajah Brooke* for Kuching, with incidents of rioting still occurring. The authorities finally managed to regain control of the situation with the help of military troops on Wednesday. By then we were far out at sea, well on our way to Sarawak for our new life together as husband and wife.

The voyage was far from being a romantic honeymoon cruise for us. As deck passengers we did not have a proper cabin but were given places to lie down, with canvas partitions providing a degree of privacy when we wanted to sleep. Despite the fact that this was my third trip on the boat, I still had not found my sea legs but took comfort that Wei was around to look after me this time, though I must say she was looking a little green as well.

I was still staying at Reservoir Road and Wei moved in there with me. A month later she found a teaching job with Chung

Hwa Chinese School. We had barely settled into the routine of matrimonial life when a familiar face appeared at our doorstep. It was Khoo with his wife and three-year-old daughter in tow. He had evacuated his family from Seremban for their safety and was now here to take up my offer of a job. I couldn't just send him away to look for his own accommodation—as his sponsor I was responsible for him. So I arranged for my rented room to be shared by having a carpenter erect a dividing wall and create separate entrances. What had been a relatively spacious room of twenty feet by ten feet for two people now had two families squeezed into it. Friends have to stick close together.

In November of 1951 Wei gave birth to our son at Kuching General Hospital. The boy was nicknamed Jolly, for as a baby he was a perpetually smiling. Jolly was initially looked after by a Malay woman during the day since Wei was teaching. Later we hired two Chinese girls, one as a nanny and the other to cook for the family and handle the household chores. My parents were both approaching their eighties and I wanted to bring my new family to pay respects to them.

By August of the following year we felt that Jolly was old enough to travel and we took the boat to Singapore. During the trip, Wei had the unenviable dual burden of attending to the needs of a ten–month-old baby and soothing a forty-one-year-old husband who was as sick as a dog. In a way that was a blessing in disguise because she didn't have time to dwell on her own discomfort. If you have never experienced the debilitating effects of seasickness, then you are indeed fortunate. You can't eat because you can't keep your food down and even the mere scent of varnished wood, or a whiff of the engine fumes, can trigger off another bout of vomiting. I once heard this joke told by a Frenchman at a dinner party, which perfectly described the miserable and pathetic condition I was in:

A ship's steward came across a passenger with an extreme case of mal de mer and tried to cheer him up by saying that he had not seen anyone die from seasickness. To which the wretched passenger gasped, "Please … the hope of dying is the only thing that's keeping me alive!"

Lau met us at Clifford Pier and kindly offered us lodging at his home where we stayed for a few days before leaving for Seremban by bus. The long, bumpy ride was interrupted by frequent stops at police checkpoints, for the Malayan Emergency was still in force. Bus passengers were prohibited from bringing along any food, especially milk powder and biscuits, lest these might find their way into the hands of the Communists. The restriction also applied to medicines and this included Western, as well as traditional Chinese medicine. As a concession, couples travelling with their babies were allowed to bring along one bottle of milk.

When the bus made its single rest stop at a village coffee shop, all the passengers spilled out in mad rush: for the weary it was a chance to stretch their legs; for those who were hungry it was a

Jolly wondering whether Wak-Wak should have a haircut like his.

chance to have a quick bite to eat; and, of course, there was a long queue for the toilet. We were a little nervous during the journey as stories had been circulating about how the Communists would sometimes emerge from the jungle and attack vehicles travelling on the main road. Fortunately, nothing like that happened and we arrived safely in Seremban where Jolly was introduced to his grandparents and the rest of the family for the first time.

When Jolly was about three years old, I bought a baby gibbon for twenty dollars to keep as a pet, along with the dog and cat that were already part of the household. This particular gibbon had grey hair—instead of the usual black colour—and a white face. The natives refer to these animals as "wak-waks", a term which, out of habit, we conveniently used as its name even though it was as creative as calling a dog "Doggie" or a cat "Kitty". We fed it milk and bananas and by the time it was six months old it was tame enough to be allowed to roam inside the house without its chain. Wak-Wak loved to climb up to the rafters of the kitchen roof where he caught spiders for snacks. However, he was not fully domesticated and to Wei's great annoyance, indiscriminately splattered the floor with his droppings when he was up in the rafters. She resorted to caning the hapless creature whenever it dirtied the kitchen floor. Wak-Wak could not understand why he was being punished for doing what was natural. He did understand that he didn't like Wei, so every time she passed by he would instantly turn around, bend over and thrust his backside at her before scampering away with a triumphant shriek!

My first son, Casey, joined us in Kuching after passing his Senior Cambridge and later went over to Sydney, Australia, for further studies. He had a notion to take up engineering and ended up doing civil engineering by default as the impressionable lad had been misled into believing that mechanical engineering involved nuts-and-bolts work of fixing car engines. How Casey found his way to Australia even though I couldn't afford to send him at that time, his lean and hungry days at the boarding house and his misspent hours of hustling in the pool halls when his university exams were just round the corner, I leave for him to tell his children.

Showdown

I had to deal with the problem of touting by gangsters again. The irony was that it actually began with the elimination of another problem. A gang of young Hokkien Chinese ran a gambling game on the pavement right in front of the Lilian. It involved placing bets—ranging from one to ten dollars—on which one of three cards being shuffled about was the King. It was similar to the game of three shells and a pea, involving sleight of hand. Fellow conspirators posing as customers would reel in the curious and the cautious with some initial wins to show how easy it was to make money. The game was called Ah-Pek Baya, or King Pays. In a reversal of eponymous convention, the gang was called the Ah-Pek Baya gang.

I have nothing against gambling activities, having worked at a gambling stall myself, albeit under extenuating circumstances, but I didn't think it was appropriate to have this distraction right on the doorstep of my cinema. I got the police to put a stop to it but the unintended effect was to turn the gang's attention to touting as an alternative. It was something they had not thought of doing before, and turned out to be more lucrative as most shows were fully sold out.

Their modus operandi was to crowd the box office the minute it opened for business and snap up thirty tickets each. With about a dozen of them doing this, it meant that close to half of the total seats in the Lilian were being resold at black-market prices. I had created my own monster! I tried to apply a solution similar to the one I'd used in Malacca—by limiting the number of tickets sold to each gang member. Unfortunately this was not Malacca and the situation was different. The gangsters became so infuriated when they found out they couldn't buy more than four tickets each that they stormed into the cinema and began thrashing the place. The show hadn't commenced yet but I quickly ordered the door-keepers to close the exits and the operator to start the film, hoping that the darkness would confound and hamper the vandals whilst I made an urgent call to the police.

Shortly, I heard a vehicle screeching to a halt and expected to see a dozen policemen armed with batons rushing into the foyer, eager to root out the miscreants. Instead I was greeted by the sight of an English inspector and his lone Gurkha sidekick strolling in casually. The Gurkhas from Nepal are known for their fierceness in combat and are regularly employed by the British military and police services. After being apprised of the situation by me, the inspector borrowed a torch and instructed the Gurkha to first take off his hat, then follow him inside the darkened auditorium. I was left perplexed. What were they were up to? When the two of them finally emerged, the inspector handed me the Gurkha's hat which was filled with money. What transpired was that the inspector had gone round, shone the torch at each person and asked to see a ticket. Those without tickets—mainly the gangsters and perhaps a few bona fide cinemagoers who had managed to sneak in—had to drop the correct amount of cash into the hat.

"That's all I can do for you," said the inspector before departing. If the gangsters had been infuriated before, they were now incensed. The minute the inspector left they sought me out and challenged me to a fight.

"Meet us at the Botanical Gardens at 10.00 am tomorrow, if you dare!"

I knew that I had no choice but to take up the gauntlet otherwise they would never leave me alone. It was obviously foolhardy to face an entire gang on my own, so I turned to my staff and asked for volunteers. Khoo, my assistant manager at the Sylvia, was more than willing to stand by my side whilst Ah-Lee, the ticket collector, also stepped forward. The rest understandably

Showdown at the Botanical Gardens.

demurred. When Khoo and I returned home, we discretely omitted to mention the appointment we had at the Botanical Gardens to our wives.

The next day we met up with Ah-Lee at 9.30 am to confer on strategy. It was agreed that we would not exacerbate the situation by arming ourselves with makeshift weapons and that we would try to watch each other's backs. After that we walked over to one of the resting sheds and sat down to wait. The sun was not at its zenith but we were already feeling the heat. I was grateful for the presence of Khoo and Ah-Lee. I didn't know Ah-Lee well but he seemed like someone who could hold his own whilst Khoo, of course, had fought in the war and was unperturbed. As for me, I didn't think that my boyhood scraps counted for much in my current situation. At ten o'clock sharp, the gangsters made their appearance. We stood up and faced the dozen or so men who surrounded us at a distance, circling like baleful-eyed predators, occasionally hurling taunts and insults. My two companions and I glared back and refused to be drawn out from our defensive position. Although they outnumbered us, we were not cowed and I daresay we must have looked like a formidable trio—a tall, strapping cinema manager with his calm, wiry assistant and a sturdy stout-hearted ticket collector. This face-off went on for at least ten minutes, although it seemed much longer as we waited tensely for them to rush at us. But as suddenly as they'd appeared, the gangsters melted away and the expected melee never materialised.

Over celebratory drinks at the coffee shop, we tried to figure out the puzzling behaviour of the gangsters. Ah-Lee boasted that they were afraid of us. I chuckled at that suggestion.

"There were so many of them and only three of us. How could they be afraid?"

Khoo had a different interpretation. By not brandishing any weapons, we had thrown our opponents into confusion for they didn't know whether they were facing very brave or very foolish men. We must have surely known that they would be out in force. Since it didn't make sense, the gangsters must have concluded that we were neither brave nor foolish but had surreptitiously alerted the police who were hiding nearby, ready to sweep in should they attack us. I saw where Khoo was heading with his reasoning: erring on the side of caution, the hoodlums must have decided to withdraw rather than risk arrest and being thrown in jail.

We laughed not only at the absurdity of the convoluted logic but also in relief, as we had primed ourselves for a bloody fight. Strangely enough, even though we had not really settled the issue with the gangsters they never bothered us after that. Which made me wonder: had someone really tipped off the police?

Episode 6

Rice Wine and Dancing Girls

Of the various indigenous tribes in Sarawak, the Ibans form the largest group. Inhabiting the coastal areas and main waterways, they are also known as Sea Dayaks and historically had a fearsome reputation as pirates and headhunters. The relatively more peace-loving Bidayuh comprise the second-largest group and can be found at the foothills of mountains with their longhouses usually sited a few hours walk from the nearest road or river. They were called Land Dayaks by the Europeans to differentiate them from their Sea Dayak cousins and have a reputation for making excellent rice wine as well as being versatile in concocting fermented drinks from sugarcane and wild mangosteen.

Jungle Virgin

Hong, the assistant manager of Lilian cinema, had a friend who regularly dropped by the office for a chat. His name was Poh, an affable man in his thirties with a chubby face and a ready smile. His family ran a thriving export business, shipping pepper and other local produce overseas—mainly to Singapore—and Poh often toured the outlying areas to source for goods. This also gave him an excellent opportunity to explore and visit the renowned Sarawak longhouses. Poh offered to bring me to a longhouse, promising an unforgettable experience. Fascinated by tales of these communal dwellings that could house the entire village under one roof, I didn't need much persuading and scheduled a trip with Poh.

On the appointed day we boarded a bus that took us down Serian Road leading south-east away from town. About fourteen miles out, we disembarked in front of a simple shack in the middle of nowhere. It was a Chinese provision shop where Poh purchased

Arriving at the Dayak Village.

six bottles of *arak* (a distilled spirit), biscuits, cigarettes and sweets from the proprietor.

"Customary to bring along something and the sweets are for the children." Poh's explanation accounted for the shop's existence, for it marked the second phase of our journey and the last chance to stock up on gifts. Carrying our newly acquired load, we followed a narrow gravel path that wound lazily past plantations with their orderly rows of pepper vines clinging to tall ironwood poles, before ending abruptly at the edge of a jungle thick with trees and undergrowth. Without pause, Poh pressed on and I quickened my pace to keep up. I didn't fancy being lost in the jungle and Poh obviously knew the way. For nearly two hours we followed a muddy track, crossing numerous gullies, until we emerged from the cover of the forest canopy into a clearing next to a small stream. I felt as if we had just gone through a sauna. My sweat-soaked shirt was plastered against my body and drops of perspiration ran freely down my brow. But we had arrived! Fanning myself with my hat, I paused to take in the sight of the solitary longhouse across the stream.

What struck me was the length of the wooden structure that easily stretched to 150 feet. It rested on stilts that rose six to eight feet high and a round log with deep notches cut into it served as the stairway. A wide verandah fronted the entire house and gave access to the partitioned rooms of individual families. Each room had its own door and window facing the verandah. The length of a longhouse was determined by the number of families living in it, and I estimated that this one had close to twenty.

The first thing Poh did was to locate the longhouse headman. Conversing in Malay—the common language between them—he requested shelter for the night and handed over the gifts we had brought, adding some money for good measure. The headman nodded and barked out orders to those present to spread the word that they were entertaining guests that evening.

With the formalities taken care of, Poh and I washed ourselves at the stream before retiring to the longhouse verandah. Several pigs were wandering about freely in front of the house

Washing up in the jungle stream.

whilst chickens darted between the stilts, pecking at the ground. As twilight descended over the rustic scene, we were served a simple meal of chicken and rice that we ate sitting on the floor. Some of the Dayak women had begun covering another section of the verandah with rattan mats in preparation for the evening's festivity. I noticed that the strips of wood making up the verandah floor were loosely fitted whilst those for the rooms were tightly joined. This was meant to facilitate household cleaning since by sweeping outwards from the room onto the verandah any dust and dirt, as well as food debris, would fall through the gaps; which explained the chickens foraging under the house.

By nightfall the rest of the villagers had returned from their toil in the distant jungle clearings where they grew rice, yam, sugarcane and other subsistence crops, but the two of us still had to wait for another hour—giving everyone a chance to rest, bathe and eat —before we were invited to sit on the mats that had been laid out earlier. We were joined by the headman and other male Dayaks, some carrying cylindrical drums. A bowl of *tuak* (rice wine) appeared and was passed around. It had to be re-filled a number of times as each person took a generous mouthful from it before handing it on. I felt queasy about quaffing from the communal bowl after seeing the badly stained teeth of some of the drinkers. Not wishing to give offence, I lifted the bowl to my mouth but made sure I covered it with both his hands, and then passed it to Poh who gave a knowing smile at my legerdemain.

Young women started to drift in and when at least half a dozen had gathered, the headman signalled for the music to start. Drumbeats filled the air. Going by turn, sometimes in a pair, the maidens would glide to the centre and perform a traditional dance. The married women watched from the sidelines whilst those young maidens who were not pre-occupied at that moment brought servings of *tuak* to us and tried to entice us to join in the dance. We politely declined, knowing that we would only make fools of ourselves with our clumsy attempts at imitating the graceful performers, and were content to watch and be entertained. The younger male Dayaks had no such inhibitions and soon joined in the fun. The merrymaking went on for two hours and by then the revellers had consumed all the alcohol we had brought for the festivity.

We were shown to an empty room where we slept on mats under mosquito nets. Or at least I tried to sleep. My mind was still actively assimilating the remarkable experiences of the day, and I spent a restless night wishing for my familiar camp bed to lie on. I was so glad when the cock's crow signalled daybreak. After washing our faces at the stream, we thanked the headman and took our leave.

I had been impressed by the warmth and sincerity of the Dayaks, but in my naïveté did not realise that their hospitality extended beyond feasting and drinking until I was enlightened by my guide as we retraced our steps. According to Poh, one could approach any of the single women to "borrow her mosquito net". If she agreed, it meant that she was willing to spend the night with that person. Protocol required that the "lucky" man present the girl with some gift, such as a bottle of perfume or small items of jewellery. Poh then went on to sternly warn me never to mistakenly pose the question to a married woman or I would lose my head! I was sure that Poh was being facetious when he told me all this. In any case, the practice of taking heads as trophies was curtailed by the White Rajahs in the late 19th century and virtually disappeared in the early 20th century. It did remind me, though, of the rattan baskets I had seen hanging on the posts when we'd first climbed up to the verandah. Each contained three or four grinning skulls—gruesome trophies of past headhunting expeditions—with short tufts of hair still attached to some of the skulls, which seemed unusual since Dayaks normally wore their hair long. When I shared this observation with Poh, the latter speculated that the heads belonged to Japanese soldiers killed by Dayaks during the war—which meant they were recent additions, less than a decade old! On reaching the Chinese provision shop, we ordered coffee and biscuits for breakfast as we waited for the bus that would take us back to Kuching and a much-needed shower!

Diamond Dutch

A few months later a stranger came by the office looking for me.

He was passing through Kuching on business and didn't want to miss out on the unique Sarawak longhouse experience before he left. He had it on good authority—from a mutual acquaintance—that I was quite the expert, having recently been to a longhouse. Two thoughts flashed through my mind: "I've been set up by my club chums," followed by "I need Poh!"

Once Poh's availability had been confirmed, arrangements were swiftly made for the trip to take place the very next day. I had difficulty pronouncing the stranger's name, but since he was from Holland I called him The Dutchman, or just Dutch for short. Dutch didn't seem to mind. He said he was a diamond trader but his somewhat shabby, ill-fitting clothes seemed to belie the veracity of that claim. Any doubts vanished when Dutch requested the use of my office safe to store his "merchandise" for the duration of the trip. He brought out two packets. From one spilled dozens of small, glittering diamonds about the size of a pinhead. Dutch made a careful count as he dropped each one back into the packet. He next pulled out a small weighing scale from his pocket and poured the contents of the second packet onto the scale until he had a twinkling heap of diamonds as tiny as grains of salt. After taking two or three readings, he poured these miniscule diamonds back into the packet. The two packets were then given to me and I slipped both into a large envelope that was ceremoniously sealed before being deposited in the office iron safe. Dutch wanted to know how many people had access to the safe and was told that there were only two sets of keys, one held by me and the other by Hong. This seemed to reassure Dutch.

Poh took us on the same route as previously—a bus ride to the provision shop followed by a trek past pepper plantations—before threading through the rainforest to the longhouse. The headman greeted us like old friends and in the evening there was the usual drinking and dancing. Dutch, who had been briefed beforehand, successfully "borrowed the mosquito net" of a heavily built maiden with a dusky complexion, underscoring the aphorism that beauty lies in the eye of the beholder. Next morning Dutch was beaming like a lighthouse as we made our way back to civilisation. Politeness kept our curiosity in check, and Poh and I never found out exactly what presents Dutch had given the girl.

The minute we got back to Kuching the packets of diamonds were taken out from the iron safe and returned to Dutch who meticulously inspected the contents, weighing the grains of diamond several times to ensure that a pinch had not been slyly siphoned off. This earned a rebuke from me: "If you don't trust us, you should have deposited your precious diamonds in the bank!" Dutch hastily apologised for any unintentional aspersions cast as a consequence of his paranoia. Expressing his gratitude for all the help rendered, he shook my hands and we parted without rancour.

The natural beauty of a Dayak maiden.

Bare Geography

I never heard from Dutch again. However, barely a year passed before yet another stranger called at the Lilian. I was working at my desk and looked up in surprise when my assistant manager ushered in a portly gentleman who ominously introduced himself as Chung, from the Corrupt Practices Investigation Bureau of Hong Kong. However, Chung's visit had nothing to do with his line of work: he was on a personal mission. As an amateur geographer, it was his keen desire to become a full-fledged member of the Geographical Society of London – better known as the

Royal Geographical Society—that had brought him to Kuching. To qualify he needed to show proof that he had undertaken some related endeavour—a field exploration or close contact with a primitive tribe. Chung had pondered over this for a while before hitting upon the idea of having himself photographed with bare-breasted tribal women in the land of headhunters. This would surely gain him admittance to the Society's inner sanctum! When he sought advice from a Hong Kong friend who had been to Kuching before, my name came up. I silently swore never to brag about my longhouse trips to anyone again. I was paid to be a cinema manager not a tourist guide!

The real expert, Poh, was consulted. We couldn't go back to the same longhouse that we'd visited twice before. Since it was relatively close to civilisation, the women in that village had adopted the sartorial convention of the town folk by being fully clothed. We had to venture much deeper into the interior to encounter Dayak women who still went au naturel from the waist up. Chung was in luck as Poh had come across such a longhouse community on one of his forays to the hinterland, but he warned that it would be an arduous journey. Chung was undeterred, confidently declaring that he was prepared to brave any hardship and then, continuing in an apologetic tone, begged for a small favour. Carried away by his wildfire idea, he had rushed all the way from Hong Kong and forgotten to bring a camera! I didn't own a camera but promised I would borrow one for the trip.

Once again we took the bus out of town, but instead of alighting at the provision shop, we rode for another six miles before Poh called out to the driver to let us off. As the vehicle lurched off noisily in a haze of dust and exhaust fumes, we split up the gifts we had brought along so that the burden would be equally shared. Poh didn't believe in hiring porters even though Chung had agreed to bear all expenses. With Poh leading the way, we stepped off the deserted road and plunged into the rainforest. It was a blur of thick undergrowth, foliage and trees as we plodded on for what seemed like an eternity. Poh guided us unerringly along the tortuous and near-invisible jungle trail, whilst I concentrated on putting one foot in front of the other and was thankful for the few short rest breaks in-between. Chung did not complain about the daunting pace, although he was sweating profusely, for he realised that Poh was trying to get us there well before sunset whilst there was still enough light for day photography. It took us over three hours before we reached our destination.

The Dayak village was larger than what I'd expected, with not just one but three longhouse buildings located near a river. Chung could hardly contain his excitement for he could see that practically all the women in the village were going about topless. Poh approached the headman and, after handing over the gifts, made the special request on Chung's behalf. The headman obliged by summoning some of the young girls over, indicating to Chung that he could take his pick. Chung made his selection and fussed over how the girls should pose next to him. As I fumbled with the camera, he badgered me about whether I was sure the pictures would turn out alright, insisting that extra shots be taken just to be on the safe side. I assured Chung that I would do my best and started snapping away to stem Chung's nervous verbal tirade. At the end of it, a delighted Chung dug up some money from his pocket and distributed it to the co-operative native "models".

With our goal accomplished, the three of us settled down to a meal of rice, chicken and some curry dishes. Despite a raging thirst, Chung was afraid to drink the water provided with the meal, accustomed as he was to city life and niceties like water on tap. Since our own limited supply of drinking water had long been exhausted during the trek to the village, Poh suggested coconut juice as an alternative. Chung thought this was acceptable, not that he had much choice. Our hosts produced several young coconuts with their tops lopped off and Chung gulped down his fill.

The advent of the evening's entertainment brought out the drums and dancing girls, as well as the communal bowl of *tuak*. Chung, wary of imbibing anything that might upset his genteel constitution, did not drink from it. Much later, after the party had wound down, we were brought to our sleeping quarters. It had been a long day and we were looking forward to a good night's rest. It seemed to me that I had hardly closed my eyes when I felt somebody shaking me. The luminous rays of dawn prying into the room revealed that it was Chung who had woken me. The man was clutching his stomach and in desperate need to get to a toilet. "Bad tummy ache—think it was the coconut juice," gasped Chung, his face contorted.

I didn't know the location of the toilet or whether they even had one. Aside from discrete visits to the bushes to empty my bladder, I was wont to withhold weightier matters till we were back in town. Coming out of the room, I spotted a male Dayak on the verandah and asked for the toilet. The native pointed in the direction of a small hut on stilts some distance away. Chung did not wait for me to explain but scampered down and rushed off in the general direction indicated, frantically searching for what he imagined should be a ground toilet facility. Not finding anything resembling an outhouse and unable to control his bowels any longer, he dashed to a nearby tree, yanked down his trousers and squatted down. He exhaled a huge sigh of relief and was in the midst of purging his bowels when he was interrupted by a loud grunting noise. Turning to the source, Chung's eyes widened at the sight of a large, grimy pig aggressively advancing towards him. Fearing that it was going to attack, he grabbed a fallen branch to fend it off but Chung's heroic sentiments segued into panic when he spotted several more pigs also moving rapidly in his direction. Being overwhelmed by a porcine horde with his pants drooped around his ankles was hardly befitting a would-be member of the Royal Geographical Society, so he flung the branch away, grabbed his pants and ran for his life, screaming for help at the top of his voice. This drew bemused glances from the villagers, who wondered why one of their guests was making such a loud fuss over domesticated pigs sniffing for slop. I chortled at this comical sight.

Struggling to contain my mirth, I came down from the verandah and went over to calm Chung. In a breathless voice,

Posing with a Dayak headman.

Chung asked for toilet paper in order to clean himself and was stupefied when I said there was none. But I did point helpfully to the nearby river. Swearing colourfully in Cantonese and still clutching his pants, Chung stumbled towards the river.

After Chung had regained his composure, if not his dignity, we said our farewells and headed back to Kuching. Chung flew back to Hong Kong, leaving me to develop and print the photos. They weren't of National Geographic magazine standard but I thought the photos turned out quite well and despatched them to Hong Kong. Some months later Chung wrote back to thank both me and Poh for all our help and proudly announced that he had been accepted into the Royal Geographic Society!

The trip with Chung was to be my last and most memorable visit to a longhouse. I had satisfied my curiosity the first time and the subsequent two occasions had really been to oblige others. In any case, events were unfolding that would unexpectedly hold hostage my free time to public service.

Of Duty and Service

After the war, the chairman of the Kuching Municipal Board was asked to study the possibility of converting the Kuching Municipality into a local government entity capable of managing its own affairs. Many of the recommendations and suggestions contained in his report were incorporated in the Kuching Municipal Bill that was later approved in 1952 and officially became the Kuching Municipal Ordinance. Thus the Kuching Municipal Council operating under its own ordinance became a separate entity from other local authorities and it did not waste any time in getting things moving.

Your Obedient Servant

At the close of 1952, I was told that I had been nominated to serve in the newly independent Kuching Municipal Council. The council was to comprise a chairman and twenty-four representatives of the public. The chairman and six councillors were appointed by the governor whilst the remaining eighteen councillors could be nominated by the associations looking after the interests of various ethnic communities. At that time I was already a committee member in the Chinese Chamber of Commerce, an Honorary Treasurer of the Kuching A.A.A. (Amateur Athletic Association), and also the Honorary English Secretary of the Kwong Wai Siu Association (a Cantonese association). I had somehow been manoeuvred into taking up these positions and in such a small community it was not easy to say no, especially since it was apparent I was going to be sticking around Kuching for a while. However, the Municipal Council was a different league from the associations and I harboured conflicting feelings about taking on the responsibility of a councillor. One of my concerns was how my employers would react to me holding an official

Swearing in, Kuching Municipal Council.

public position—albeit an unpaid one—at the same time that I was working for them. Prudence had me dash off a letter to Dato Loke in Singapore, sounding him out on the matter. It wasn't until I transferred to Kuching that I began to have more contact with Dato Loke, since I was the "man in the field", and occasionally had to consult him on business matters as well as look after him whenever he came to visit or officiate the opening of cinemas.

Dato Loke came from a large and wealthy family and was the ninth of eleven children of Loke Yew, a self-made millionaire and a well-known figure in Malaya. An Honours graduate in English Literature and History, he was pulled into the cinema business by his mother, Mrs Loke Yew, and became the driving force of Cathay which he built into an empire. He pursued his hobbies with the same passion and vigour, and was a respected ornithologist and photographer of birds. There was much to admire about this talented man who was four years younger than me but had already achieved so much in his life. Dato Loke wrote back to me on Christmas Eve saying:

I was very happy to learn from your letter of 16th December 1952 that you had been nominated a municipal councillor for Kuching. My most sincere congratulations! The members of your association have chosen wisely, and I am sure they will never regret their choice. We here in Singapore will watch your career in the council with a great deal of interest, and

139

I would be very happy to hear from you, from time to time, about your experiences in public life.

Reassured by Dato Loke's support and encouragement, I indicated my willingness to serve in the Municipal Council and promptly received a solemn notification from the Secretariat on 30th December 1952:

Sir,

I am directed to inform you that the Governor-in-Council has been pleased, under section 5 (1) of The Kuching Municipal Ordinance, 1952, to appoint you to be a member of the Kuching Municipal Council for a period of three years with effect from 1st January 1953, subject to the proviso for retirement in rotation contained in section 6 (1).

I am, Sir, Your Obedient Servant

Chief Secretary

I was placed on the Finance Committee and made vice-chairman of the General Purpose and Traffic Committee (GPAT), the description "general purpose" being a catch-all for miscellaneous matters. Each committee held meetings monthly, which meant I had two meetings to attend every month. These were held on a weekday and usually in the afternoon. On reflection, I was grateful for this gentle induction into the council for I soon discovered that committees proliferated faster than councillors, and by the following year I was sitting on no less than five council committees; the additions being the Special Works Committee (mainly public works), the Rating Appeal Committee (dealing with appeals on the rates of various municipal taxes imposed) and last but not least the Kuching Safety First Committee. Not only was I still in the GPAT but two years later I was elevated from vice-chairman to chairman!

One of the main challenges thrown to me as the GPAT chairman was to resolve the chaotic public transport situation. At that time, Kuching had one large bus company known as Chin Lian Long (CLL) and dozens of independent small buses operated by individuals. The latter were dubbed "mosquito buses" as they did not adhere to any fixed routes but buzzed around, competing for passengers among themselves as well as with CLL. The intense rivalry between the independent operators engendered a racetrack mentality, with drivers racing along the roads in order to be the first to get to the people waiting at a bus stop. Such reckless behaviour endangered lives and more often than not ended up causing accidents.

This unhappy state of affairs was exacerbated by the fact that all the buses (including those belonging to CLL) were poorly maintained and barely roadworthy. The onus fell on me and another council member to work out a solution in conjunction with the Motor Licensing Authority of the Land Transport Department.

The first step was to hold a series of separate meetings with the individual bus owners as well as CLL Bus Company to explain the Municipal Council's concerns, and at the same time get feedback from the various parties. Following this, the GPAT task force reviewed the situation and came to the conclusion that a single merged company, properly managed, would have the advantage of economy of scale and assured profitability to operate a fleet of well-maintained buses.

I called for a second round of meetings with the bus operators to table this suggestion. CLL was amenable to the idea but the independent operators had an opposing view. Even when they were scrambling for customers among themselves they still saw CLL as their main rival. From their perspective, a merger was equivalent to being sponged up by their largest competitor to become a bloated monopoly. This went against their enterprising spirit which impelled them to come up with an alternative: why not band together as a separate company and pit their combined resources against CLL? To help raise capital they would trade in their old vehicles. The fact that these individualistic operators were thinking of organising themselves was at least a step forward!

Being enamoured by the idea of taking on CLL collectively did not straight away resolve the differences of this motley collection of small-time bus operators, who descended into a quagmire of endless squabbling about the details of the new company's formation. Eventually they realised that they had fallen back to the ingrained habit of petty rivalry—as if they were still racing their buses to snatch passengers away from each other—and reached a consensus from which emerged the second Kuching bus company, the Sarawak Transport Company (STC).

Now that there were two bus companies, the next question was how to allocate the routes between them. The most compelling proposal offered the simplicity of a clean and clear division: have one company operate within the Municipality boundaries and the other outside it. Unfortunately both companies wanted the more lucrative Municipal area and this started a new round of heated discussions. Negotiations swung back and forth, peppered by a great deal of haggling. With the moderating influence of the GPAT task force, an agreement was finally reached. CLL would restrict its operations to the Municipal area whilst the fledgling STC would run the longer routes out of Kuching to Serian, Bau and other towns. This marked a new beginning for bus services in Kuching, and the fact that both companies are still extant is a testament to the lasting foundation laid by the GPAT and everyone else involved.

To Catch a Thief

It was sometime in 1953, when I was getting into the swing of things at the Municipal Council, that a shooting incident occurred near Bau, a gold mining town several miles from Kuching. The Emergency was still in force and although Sarawak was relatively unaffected by events in the Malayan Peninsula, the government nevertheless felt jittery about possible Communist involvement. This seemingly unrelated event was to impact on me in the form of a phone call from the Chief of Police, who felt that Khoo's background might prove useful in their investigations and asked whether he could be spared on a temporary basis. Since it was a matter of the country's security, I told him I had no objections. Khoo, in turn, was more than willing to help, finding it amusingly ironic that his MPAJA past, which had always cast a shadow on his life, was now viewed as a potential source of illumination.

Thereafter, twice weekly in the evenings, Khoo reported to Police Headquarters where he pored over various documents that the police believed were related to the infiltration of Communists into Sarawak, translating them from Chinese to English. Having lived in the Malayan jungle with the Communists, he was also grilled for his knowledge about their modus operandi. This continued for four months before Khoo returned to his normal life. It wasn't going to stay normal for very long.

One day Khoo approached me for advice. His co-operation and insights had impressed the authorities and he was being offered a permanent job with the police force: should he take it? I told Khoo that he had to make his own choices but assured him that I would not stand in the way, either as his boss or as his sponsor, if joining the police was what he really wanted to do. Khoo mulled over it and in the following year signed up with the

Sarawak Police. He was immediately given the rank of inspector, a testimony to how much his experience and skills were valued. Khoo applied himself sedulously to his work and it seemed he had found his calling. Sent to London for training, he was awarded the Baton of Honour for outstanding performance in his course. Khoo and his family continued to stay with us, even after we moved out of Reservoir Road to a larger rented house in Green Road where the families had proper separate rooms. But once he signed up with the Force, he and his family moved out to the government quarters that were provided for police personnel. In the late 1950s Khoo was seconded to Sibu and put in charge of the entire Third Division (territory) of Sarawak. He was later transferred back to Kuching as Assistant Commissioner in the early 1960s. Khoo remained very much a wanted man by the police force!

I was able to keep track of Khoo's progress through news reports about his official appointments. Our divergent career paths and busy lives prevented us from meeting until almost a decade and a half later, in the early 1970s, when our schedules permitted us to get together once in a while for a re-union of sorts. I remembered the very last occasion I was with Khoo; we were having lunch at the Cathay Restaurant in Singapore and both of us talked more than we ate, updating each other on news about family and friends whilst cracking jokes in between about the "good old days". I congratulated Khoo on his achievements and remarked that he had done extremely well for himself in

Sarawak. This led Khoo to mention that there was possibility he might be transferred to Malaya in the future. I pointed out that the Communists in Malaya had never rescinded their death sentence on him and expressed concern for his safety.

"If you can, continue to stay in Sarawak, out of their reach," I cautioned. But Khoo must have felt that the danger had faded with the passage of time. The Malayan Emergency was officially declared over in 1960, with the remnants of the Communist elements having surrendered or scattered across the Thai border. Even if he was wrong, he would have considered the call of duty a stronger imperative than some disquiet about personal safety.

And so when the time came, Khoo accepted his transfer to Ipoh to become the Perak Chief of Police. Perak was the state where the killing of the plantation managers by Communist elements had triggered the Malayan Emergency. It seemed that the Communists were indeed a spent force, for two years passed and nothing happened to Khoo. Then in November 1975, whilst Khoo was being driven in his official car—a distinct white Volvo—two motorbikes began to trail it. When the Volvo slowed to a stop at a red light, the bikers drew abreast of the vehicle, whipped out their guns and pumped countless rounds of bullets into it. Khoo was rushed to the Ipoh hospital but could not be saved for his wounds were fatal. The Communists have a long memory.

I was saddened by the news of Khoo's death. It seemed ironic that he had fled from the jaws of death over twenty years before only to return to its unforgiving maws. Khoo was conferred the title of Tan Sri (the second most senior title after Tun) posthumously for his exemplary service and sacrifice in combating communist terrorism. His body was returned to Seremban for burial at the Sekamat cemetery. Coincidentally it was also where my father was buried, and on those occasions when I visited my father's grave, I would walk across the path over to Khoo's gravestone to pay my respects to an extraordinary man who had once been my colleague, roommate, subordinate and most of all, my friend.

Minor Miracle

Following my appointment as councillor, I felt that befitting my status as an "important" public official, I should actually own a car. It may seem a bit vain on my part, but to have risen in social

Latest addition to the family—the Morris Minor.

147

standing from a lowly clerk to a city councillor, I think, deserved a reward. My driving licence was obtained in Seremban before the war, not because I had anticipated owning a car, for such a prospect had seemed extremely unlikely at that time, but so that I could borrow Chen's (or rather, his father's) Austin for little escapades to Port Dickson. Having set my mind to purchase a car, I imagined that it would be such a grand feeling being able to drive around town whenever I needed to or whenever I felt like going for a spin. But I soon realised that I couldn't afford a brand new vehicle and had to content myself with something second-hand.

After a brief search I found a black, two-door Morris Minor which had definitely seen better years. It was supposedly at the bargain price of $800 which still set me back by more than a month's salary. The car needed extensive repairs to the body and the engine but luckily I knew a mechanic, who agreed to undertake the work "at cost" as a favour to me. It took him an entire week to restore the vehicle. It had to be stripped down, parts replaced, re-assembled again and the engine finely tuned. When the Morris was finally returned to me, it was totally transformed and I couldn't believe it was the same one that I had brought to him. It had been washed and polished till it gleamed like a showroom piece.

Sliding into the driver's seat, I was even more astonished when I started the engine for it purred like a kitten without any of the shuddering fits that had plagued it previously. I praised the mechanic for the fantastic makeover job. He grinned with pride but modestly admitted that, given the state of the vehicle's disrepair, it was actually a miracle that he'd managed to get it back into shape at all!

Now that I was the proud owner of a good-as-new Morris Minor, I dropped Wei off at school every day before going to work. Wei was so elated by the "luxury" of us actually owning a car that she expressed a keen desire to take up driving. I couldn't say no and arranged for a driving instructor to give her lessons in the Morris. Some time passed, then one day the instructor came to me and declared with diplomatic exasperation that Wei was as ready as she would ever be for her driving test. Wei took her test and passed the first time round. Of course, it was tangential that driving tests came under the authority of the Kuching Municipality and that I was a member of the Traffic Committee.

It was inevitable that where you found a Cathay cinema, you would also find a Shaw cinema and vice versa as both competed in the same markets. Shaw actually had the lead in penetrating Borneo and planted its flag in Sandakan, Jesselton and all over Sarawak much earlier than Cathay. Shaw had two cinemas in Kuching in the early 1950s (Lido and Rex) that were in much better condition than the Sylvia and Lilian. Ming, their general manager (for Borneo territories) but based in Kuching, was proud of this fact and was at pains to point out to all and sundry that his cinemas were newer and more modern than the Sylvia and Lilian. I took this criticism in my stride as there was no denying the fact and I didn't see any point in engaging in a war of words.

However, hearing it repeatedly grated the nerves of some of my friends, especially two of old man Yap's sons whom I got to know quite well. They were upset by Ming's braggadocio but more so by my nonchalance to what they perceived as an insult to me. The hotheads took it on themselves to confront Ming, and make threatening noises. The denigrating remarks about Cathay cinemas did stop but it was more likely a result of it having become a tired tune.

Despite the intense rivalry between Cathay and Shaw, there was never any personal animosity between staff on both sides. Ming and I were 'friendly competitors' and not just in Kuching, for I had been promoted to the position of Supervisor of Sarawak, Brunei and North Borneo in late 1954, and hence we were more or less covering the same territories. In fact, I was once even invited to Ming's home where I discovered another side to his character. He had a passion for flowers and had a splendid collection of orchids gathered from various parts of Borneo.

If there was any competition, it was for poster space. Movies were advertised in the local newspapers but our man in Kuching responsible for placing those advertisements was also the poster writer. He would produce the simple wall posters using thick sheets of white paper that were hung up at designated places around town such as street corners and coffee shops, announcing the movies being shown, whilst his Shaw counterpart did the same. Sometimes in their enthusiasm, those responsible for putting the posters up would encroach on each other's territories.

Dato Loke visited Kuching on several occasions and always enjoyed the kind hospitality of the governor, now Sir Anthony Abell as he was knighted in 1952. Not only would Sir Anthony Abell insist that the Dato and his wife stay at his official residence, the Astana, but would host dinner parties there in honour of his guests. As Cathay's key representative in Sarawak, I was often invited to these formal gatherings where, weather permitting, functions were sometimes held outside in its sprawling grounds which also included a tennis court.

Getting to the Astana meant a short ride on the official motor launch directly across the Kuching River to the jetty on the opposite bank, or you could take one of the boats that ply the river, carrying passengers to and fro. It was on the occasion of Dato Loke's visit in 1955 that I was placed in a most embarrassing position by my fellow councillor, Song, who was the manager of William Jacks Limited. He was a good friend of mine and a regular but boisterous mahjong partner who loved his beer. The governor was entertaining Dato Loke at the Astana as usual, and both Song and I were among the invited guests. By this time it had become public knowledge that I was to be transferred to the capital of North Borneo, Jesselton, before the end of the year. But unbeknownst to me, Song had been deputised by certain members of the community to have a discrete word with Sir Anthony Abell regarding the great loss the council and associations would face with my impending departure. Song quietly urged the governor to do something about it, anticipating that the latter would pull Dato Loke aside at some point and, in turn, have a few quiet words with him.

Instead, the governor fired an unexpected broadside in the middle of dinner by openly questioning Dato Loke on why he was removing his ablest employee from Kuching, one who was not only highly popular with the business community but who was performing excellent public service. Our table suddenly became a frozen tableau of diners; conversation ceased and silver forks with morsels of food speared at their tips paused in mid-flight towards opened mouths.

Dato Loke was absolutely taken aback and for once was at a loss for words. With his eyebrows quizzically arched above his black-rimmed spectacles, he turned to me. I choked on my food and wondered whether this faux pas was going to cost me my career—Dato Loke must be thinking that I had engineered this incident in order to pressure him to change his mind about moving me! Breaking the awkward silence, Sir Anthony Abell fielded the question to me and asked me how I felt about being transferred. It gave me a chance to try and salvage the situation. Groping for an answer, my mind hurtled back to a few months before when I'd first been informed that I had to relocate. My tenure in Kuching was coming to six years; long enough to establish many close ties. It was not just on the social front. My active involvement with the associations and Municipal Council made me very much a part of Kuching, if Song's well-intentioned but foolish attempt to derail my departure was any indicator. So why was I willing to leave?

I put it simply to the governor that Cathay was still continuing to expand and that it was my duty to go where I was needed, even though I was sad about leaving Kuching. Sir Anthony Abell didn't press the matter further and Dato Loke seemed pleased with my answer. The tension evaporated and dinner returned to its former conviviality. After I learnt what had happened behind the scenes, I gave Song a severe verbal drubbing when we next met up for one of our mahjong sessions.

"You can't blame me for trying!" he retorted. "Anyway, that was a facile answer you gave to Sir Tony. Now tell me, really, why are you deserting all your friends?"

As far as I was concerned, I had spoken the truth.

And so in October 1955, I said goodbye to the Land of the Dayaks. My wife and four-year-old son were to join me in Jesselton two months later. I recalled my mistake six years before, when I'd had the entry visa in my passport stamped "North Borneo" instead of "Sarawak". As it turned out it hadn't been a mistake after all—it had just been six years too early.

EPISODE 8

Land Beneath the Winds

In 1898 the British North Borneo Chartered Company (BNBCC) trading post on Gaya Island was ransacked and set ablaze by local rebels. The company decided to rebuild its trading post but to relocate it to the mainland instead, and Jesselton was established. It soon flourished as a busy centre, dealing in rubber, rattan, honey and wax and its development was helped by the fact that it was also the terminus for the trans-Borneo railway. When North Borneo became a British crown colony after the Second World War, Jesselton was made the capital.

"Jessel-town" was named after Sir Charles Jessel, Vice-Chairman of the BNBCC, but locals found the name difficult to pronounce and preferred to call it Api Api. This presumably was related to the burning of the trading post on Gaya Island: when the people on the mainland saw the great flames leaping up the sky from the island across the bay, they shouted "Api, api" which means "Fire, fire". The incident left such an imprint on the people's minds that the replacement trading post on the mainland got stuck with that unofficial name.

Clan Woes

The best thing about this transfer was that it didn't involve a sea voyage. All it took was a short plane ride and I didn't even get airsick. Whereas Kuching is a river town, Jesselton is a coastal one and it looked much more modern than the former as most of the buildings were relatively new, having been constructed after the war. Jesselton suffered double destruction when it was razed by the British when they retreated from the Japanese and then bombed by the Allies in 1945 when they came to liberate it. Only the Atkinson Clock Tower, the old General Post Office and the Welfare Building were left standing, and these dated from 1905, 1918 and 1920 respectively.

I took charge of the Odeon, a partnership cinema (like the Lilian and Sylvia of Kuching) as Cathay did not have its own

Landing at Jesselton Airport.

cinema in Jesselton at that time. But it was my role as supervisor that kept me busy. I had to make regular inspection trips to Cathay-owned cinemas; distribute films to the independent cinemas in the smaller towns; recruit staff for new cinemas being set up, and organise and officiate the opening of cinemas not only in North Borneo but towns in Sarawak (Miri and Sibu) and Brunei (Seria). This had me travelling quite a bit.

In leaving Kuching I not only left behind all my good friends and colleagues, but something of great sentimental value—my Morris Minor. It seemed a pity, but the cost of bringing it over to Jesselton would have been prohibitive. As a favour to me, one of my friends agreed to take ownership of the car and paid what I thought was an over-the-top sum of $600 for it! It was comforting to know that the Morris Minor which had served me well, with surprisingly few breakdowns, would be in good hands.

I was toying with the idea of scouting for another cheap, second-hand car when I was saved the trouble by Dato Loke. He placed a vehicle at my disposal a few months after my arrival in Jesselton by having it shipped all the way from Singapore. It was one of his fleet of company cars that had seen a few years of service and was due to be rotated if not replaced. It may have been second-hand and black like my previous car, but other than that it was like comparing chalk and cheese. What I got was a four-door Holden sedan with a powerful two-litre engine that humbled the Morris Minor's modest engine capacity of less than 1000cc. I had to curb Wei's enthusiasm and delight in thinking that she would get to drive a bigger, more prestigious car by telling her it was a company car meant for my convenience, not hers. It wouldn't seem right if she hogged its use, especially when the company was bearing all related expenses such as petrol, servicing, road tax and insurance. It was only later when I requested for and received approval to purchase a new Hillman Estate (costing about $7,000) in Jesselton, that she finally got her chance to sit behind the steering wheel once more.

The second company car was a station wagon and the main reason for getting it was that the Holden was not suitable for transporting reels of film, packed into several large trunks, for distribution to cinemas in the outlying areas beyond Jesselton. As long as the Hillman was not required for that purpose, Wei could make use of it, which she did, ferrying our son to and from school and driving herself to work at the Chung Wah Primary School at Kampung Ayer. I continued to drive the Holden.

It was whilst I was in Jesselton that my father passed away after suffering a stroke two years earlier from which he never fully recovered. He died in November 1957. The last I saw of him was in 1954, when I made my second visit to Seremban. I was still based in Kuching then and he still looked robust for an eighty-year-old man. I couldn't make it back to Seremban in time, although the rest of my siblings were present for his funeral. I regretted that I had never tried to venture past his curtain of patriarchal reticence to learn more about his early years. Life is such that we end up becoming too occupied in coping with the exigencies of the present and mapping our hopes for the future to delve into the roots of our past. All that I'm left with now are conjectures; he must have gone through some sort of schooling, for he was able to read obscure treatise on Chinese herbs and medicines and he was obviously a clever man, able to lift himself by the bootstraps to become an established dentist. But what he did before leaving China is a story that he took to his grave.

As I reflected on his time with us, vagrant pieces of memories resurfaced burnished by an adult's perspective. Through a little boy's eyes I saw him reading the Chinese classics on court intrigue and romance to my mother whilst lying down next to her on the wooden floor of the upstairs bedroom in Locke Road. The glow of the kerosene lamp between them revealed the rapt attention on my mother's face, and the tenderness in my father's voice floated across the room as he unlocked a world of words for her enjoyment.

My father knew that literacy was the key to knowledge, and whilst English had become the language of progress, Chinese was still our heritage. I have him to thank for an early childhood grounding in my mother tongue: when he learnt that an acquaintance had engaged a Chinese tutor for his son, he made me attend as well, even though he had to make special arrangements with a rickshaw driver to transport me to the acquaintance's house at eight o'clock in the morning and back at four in the afternoon. I remembered, too, that he kept a male magpie for its vocal, as well as fighting, abilities. Every morning he would remove the cloth cover that he had placed over the bamboo cage the night before and bring the magpie, which had jet-black feathers covering the neck and part of its chest, out to a nearby field where it would trill a tune in celebration of being outdoors. If other magpies were similarly gathered nearby in their cages, they would all end up in a singing competition. Occasionally my father would pit his magpie against another—usually belonging to a neighbour—in a fight and the two cages linked by the opened doors provided a convenient enclosed arena.

Once, I accidentally left the magpie's cage door open and was so afraid that I would be scolded for letting it escape. Except that it never flew away for some reason.

The magpie's favourite food was grasshoppers, and as a young boy of eight or nine I would go out and catch them because my father offered me ten cents for every hundred that I brought back. Equipped with a cage and a long cane with a loop of wire mesh at the tip, I would prowl around the golf course grounds of Government Hill. It was sweaty work and eventually my enthusiasm would wilt under the hot sun so I didn't always meet my quota. Even so, my father would take the cage of stridulant grasshoppers from me and regardless of the shortfall from the agreed number, paid me ten cents anyway.

As my father was from the county of Sin Hui in Canton province, I joined the Sze Yi Association when I first arrived in Jesselton. *Sze yi* means "four counties", comprising Sin Hui, Hoi Ping, Toi San and Yan Ping of Canton province in southern China. The Sze Yi Association is therefore a Cantonese clan association. Another Cantonese clan association is Kwong Wai Siew, comprising the counties of Kwang Chiew, Wai Chiew and Seng Heng. The latter association was the one where I was appointed the Honorary English Secretary in Kuching.

Aside from the Cantonese associations, there were also other region/dialect-based associations such as the Hokkien, Hainanese and Hakka associations. In the early days, such associations were formed all over Southeast Asia, with the primary purpose of providing succour to immigrants from the related counties. Many of these immigrants who came seeking their fortune and a new life had no friends or relatives to turn to. However, in later years, when the flow of immigrants dwindled, the associations turned their attention to providing entertainment in addition to looking after the welfare of its clan members.

Although I wasn't very active in the association and was only an ordinary member, I was approached by a representative of the committee in late 1959 who asked me to assume the chairmanship of the association. I was very flattered but declined since I was fully occupied with my work (Cathay Jesselton was due to be opened in November) and my social commitments.

"You don't understand," the representative said with a pleading note in his voice, "you've already been unanimously elected to the post by our entire committee!" I couldn't imagine why I was held in such high esteem by these officials—other than the fact that I was a senior manager with a big organisation—but thought it would be bad form for me to refuse since I had been drafted into the post anyway. It was at my first committee meeting that I realised that I had been inveigled into taking up a hot seat that nobody else wanted! The association was in serious financial trouble. A brief background is in order to understand how this deplorable state of affairs came about.

The Sze Yi Association fell dormant during the Japanese occupation but was revived in 1947. It had jurisdiction over the west coast of North Borneo with affiliated clubs in the smaller towns. Desiring its own permanent premises, a two-storey building was constructed with the upper floor devoted to its office, in-door recreation and accommodation for visiting members from out of town, whilst the ground floor was rented out to a Chinese restaurant at $400 a month. The construction cost was largely funded through bank loans and the building was officially opened on 25th November 1956.

Three years down the road, the association still had an outstanding loan of $9,000 and the bank was pounding on the door calling for the settlement of several months of overdue repayments. The association depended on its income from the monthly rent to service its instalments, whilst membership subscriptions and mahjong tax (this being a levy on members using the club premises for "friendly" games of mahjong) were used to cover overhead expenses. However, the restaurant itself was struggling to survive and was six months in arrears in rent. I had to find some other means of generating income ... and soon ... or I would gain instant notoriety as the captain at the helm of an association sunk by bankruptcy!

The Lunar New Year of the Rat was approaching and I saw an opportunity before us. The government permitted clubs and associations to apply for licences to hold open gambling during the first three days of Chinese New Year but the Sze Yi Association had never taken advantage of this because the previous committees feared it would be ruinous to its members who might gamble away their life savings. I understood the underlying concern given my past experience as a croupier in Seremban. However, our members were flocking to other clubs and associations to gamble anyway. I told the committee members since the Year of the Rat was the start of a new cycle in the Chinese zodiac, it was an appropriate time to adapt and change. I applied for the three-day gambling permit, which was duly granted to the association.

To simplify matters for ourselves, the operation of the gambling stalls was tendered out to a third party, and the bid for that first year in 1960 was $8,000. The following year it was almost doubled at $15,000. And for the next two years after that it peaked at about $20,000. The government stopped issuing gambling licences from 1964 but by then the association had not only cleared its debt but was flushed with cash, and I had part of the surplus re-invested for the association with the purchase of two small pieces of land along Race Course Road in Tanjong Ahru.

Wildest Dream

I was given an allowance by the company and that went towards

My very own house in Likas—under construction.

the rental of a small single-storey concrete house that was near the airport and opposite the racecourse. The place was stiflingly warm and plagued by flies from the stables nearby. We stayed there for a couple of years then shifted to a more salubrious abode farther up the road, nearer Tanjong Ahru Beach. My mother was now staying with us. After my father's death, the old lady only had Ching around at our family home at Locke Road: my second sister, who married a goldsmith hailing from Kuala Lumpur, had by this time moved to Singapore with her husband and three children; my brother had left Seremban straight after the war to seek his fortune in Hong Kong and ended up running his own little trading company and settling there. Ching was pre-occupied with the dental practice and wrote to me about her concern that our mother was quietly pining away in a house filled with memories of absent people. A change in environment for the old lady seemed in order.

Our second home was a fairly spacious wooden house raised on concrete stilts which not only made it more airy but provided sheltered parking below for the two cars. Because of its height, the outside stairway had quite a number of steps and could get slippery when it rained. Although my mother was in her mid-eighties, she was still sprightly and able to walk on her own unaided. Unfortunately, one day, as she was negotiating her way down the stairs, she fell and fractured her pelvic bone. She was hospitalised but complications resulted and she died in January

1960. The Sze Yi Association took care of all the arrangements for her funeral and I only had to follow the rituals. If my father's demise had evoked wistful rumination, then my mother's death recalled a forlorn feeling similar to what I had experienced as a little boy of six. My mother was busy looking after my baby sister and I had no playmates then, for there were no boys my age living next door to us and I was still too young to be allowed to roam the neighbourhood to seek companionship. The only toys I possessed were small, flat animal-shaped lead pieces that came with the folded wafer biscuits sold by hawkers, but my little zoo collection could not hold my interest forever. So I would often sit alone at the five-foot way outside our house, absorbing with a numbness of solitude, the motion of rickshaws, bicycles and bullock carts wheeling past. Watching my mother's coffin being lowered into her grave, I was filled with the numb acceptance of the inevitable cycle of life.

I was very comfortable with our second house in Tanjong Ahru and would have continued living there if not for certain events that forced me to consider the unimaginable. In 1959, an acquaintance from my hometown of Seremban decided to invest in some property in Jesselton. Just as the Land Office was ready to make the transfer, it discovered that the seller was not the actual owner. The contract was declared void which naturally upset the buyer, my acquaintance, who lodged a protest stating that it wasn't his fault and that he had entered the transaction in good faith. As it happened, there was plot of government land in Likas, outside Jesselton town, that was to be divided into eight lots. To mollify the aggrieved purchaser, the Land Office sold him two lots at a discounted price of $200 per lot, with the balance to be opened to public ballot. My Seremban acquaintance alerted me to this and Wei urged me to apply at once. I was dismissive of the idea and told her it was a waste of time. The six lots were bound to attract hundreds of local applicants and since I was a foreigner I doubted that they would even glance at my application.

Wei's insistence was likely kindled by an aspiration to become landed gentry and not because of any farsighted shrewdness regarding property investment on her part. I say this because of an incident relating to her sense of fair value that involved the Kowloon All Star Revue. The revue was a travelling Chinese vaudeville with the main attraction being its troupe of scantily clad female dancers. I had rendered the revue some assistance in getting permits for their debut tour of Sarawak and Brunei in 1954 as they had been having difficulty in getting clearance to stage what was considered a risqué performance in those days. They played to a capacity house nightly at the various towns and raked in a tidy profit.

The revue's second tour in 1956 included North Borneo, and when I met up with their tour leader she presented me with the gift of a large ruby in gratitude for my past help. From its size, I

Ladies from the Kowloon All Star Revue.

estimated that it was more than three carats. I gave the ruby to Wei who had it mounted on a ring for twenty dollars. She wore it to school and a fellow teacher was so filled with admiration for it that Wei sold it to her for thirty dollars.

The very next day the teacher rang to ask whether Wei had any more such items to sell. I remain eternally bemused and unable to understand the inner workings of my wife's mind; she really didn't need the money and surely she must have known that the tour leader would not insult me with a ten-dollar trinket. In any case I wrote in to the Land Office, more to placate Wei than with any real hope of succeeding.

Three weeks later, in September 1959, I was stunned when a

letter came from the Land Office congratulating me on a successful ballot and informing me that I had been allocated one lot of land at the price of $300. My first thought was that the Land Office must have slipped up again and it was obviously an error. When I made enquiries, I was assured that there had been no mix-up and documents relating to the land sale were all in order. I was left in a state of bewilderment until the chairman of the Jesselton Town Board rang some weeks later and enlightened me. He was convinced that my previous experience in the Kuching Municipal Council would make me a valuable addition to the Town Board. There was just one minor snag: the rules stipulated that only landowners were eligible to serve on the Board. The chairman smugly announced that since I was now a landowner, nothing stood in his way of harnessing my services. It wasn't an error after all but a conspiracy!

So the Town Board got me, and I got a piece of property 9,000 square feet in size. But there was a catch to it. The land could not just be left vacant. I had to commence building on my lot within fifteen months—the deadline was 1st March 1961—or I would forfeit it. The leasehold varied from ninety years (if the structure was fully concrete) to sixty years (if a mixture of wood and concrete were used). This was going to cost me more than I'd envisaged but how much more had yet to be determined. First, I had to have the plans drawn up for the house. Luckily, this was resolved by an architect friend who offered to do it free of charge in acknowledgement of a past favours he'd received from me.

Then I needed a contractor, so I resorted to using the same one who had worked on the construction of Cathay Jesselton. If it was good enough for Cathay, it was more than good enough for me. The contractor estimated the cost of the house would be about $35,000 but I needed to make a down payment of twenty percent before work could begin. A quick check of my liquid assets showed that I couldn't even scrape together a quarter of the required amount! The financial obstacle seemed insurmountable and it appeared that the Town Board would not have my services for long. But by now I was also caught up with the dream of owning my own house. That and the fact that Wei would never give me a moment's peace if I just let the land title lapse, having been granted it on a silver platter.

Out of desperation I sent a plea to Dato Loke, explaining the circumstances and asking for a personal loan to cover the down payment. His reply came with a cheque. I was grateful to have such an understanding boss. With the building contractor's down payment settled, I arranged to borrow $30,000 from the Borneo Housing Board with repayment stretched over fifteen years.

The plot of land was about four and half miles out of town in Likas, and construction began in early 1961. I dropped by the site from time to time and was initially puzzled by the slow progress, until I found out that most of the labourers belonged to the Sze Yi clan. Since I was the chairman of the Sze Yi Association, word had spread among the workmen that it was their leader's house they were working on and it had better be of the highest quality! Meticulous attention was paid to the smallest details: for example, planks of wood were carefully inspected and those with wormholes were discarded and replaced.

It was to take more than a year before the work was anywhere near completion. With so much care being channelled into the building of the house, I felt that we had to do our part when it came to furnishing the place. So in early 1962, I took my annual leave and together with Wei, flew over to Hong Kong to undertake some serious shopping ... for furniture. It was also an excuse for me to catch up with my younger brother and his family whom we had not seen for quite a while, and we brought Jolly along to meet his cousins for the first time. Besides the cost of the furniture there were also shipping charges and a host of miscellaneous expenses for items that I'd never had to concern myself with (such as wiring, electrical fittings, kitchen appliances, lamps, carpets and curtains) when I'd just been a rent-paying tenant. Inevitably, this whole business of putting together a house attracted the attention of the Personnel Department back in Singapore who wondered, on the basis of the salary I was earning, how I could afford such a costly endeavour. I don't blame them. In the beginning I didn't think I could pull it off either, but getting the loans were a big help. An apparatchik from the department was duly dispatched to Jesselton to investigate me. Needless to say, everything was above board and the matter was dropped.

The house was finally completed in late 1962 and we were able to move in before Christmas. It was a two-storey building with a rectangular stretch of garden at the front and back. On the ground level of the main section were the kitchen, store room and dining room, with a staircase leading up to the three bedrooms as well as the upstairs living room. The living room with its balcony jutted out perpendicularly from the main section and was supported by concrete stilts, forming a porch below where we could park both cars. It was beyond my wildest dream to find myself staying in my very own house with all the comforts I could ever want; I could even luxuriate in the coolness of my master bedroom, having succumbed to the temptation of installing an air conditioner.

The year that we moved to Likas was also memorable for another reason: earlier in May my son, Casey, graduated from Sydney University with a Bachelor of Engineering degree. I was proud of him in more ways than one, for his scholarly achievement redeemed my own unfulfilled academic potential. I only wished that my father had lived long enough to see his first grandchild become a university graduate. Casey came over to Jesselton and found a job with the Public Works Department. So, with the exception of my daughter who was living and working in Kuala Lumpur, my family was with me.

Mountain

In addition to sitting on various committees with the Town Board, I was also made chairman of the Traffic Circulation Committee, no doubt because of my experience with the GPAT committee in Kuching, which was probably the original reason why I'd been drafted onto the Town Board in the first place. A year after I arrived in Jesselton, I was invited to join the Rotary Club. I felt a resonance with the Rotary's values and became an active member, holding office as the director in charge of community service two years later.

In mid-1961 I was elected President of the Rotary Club. Ever since the founding of the Jesselton Rotary Club in 1952, every club president had to take responsibility for one or more projects that promoted the Rotary's aim of service to society. Past projects had ranged from the building of a youth club; donations of school equipment; a Road Safety Exhibition; and the beautification of Tanjong Aru Beach. Not every project could be completed during a president's term, and the responsibility for the unfinished task would be borne by the incoming president. When I took over as president, there were no outstanding projects and I was left scratching my head to come up with an idea.

That was when a member of the London Royal Society for the Blind suggested that the Rotary undertake the raising of funds to build a centre where the visually handicapped could be housed and taught handicraft skills to help them earn a living. The society did not have a branch in Jesselton and had to rely on the assistance and influence of the Rotary Club to further its goals, one of which was to eventually establish a Borneo chapter of the society.

Despite the vested interest behind the suggestion, a centre for the blind was nevertheless a splendid idea. Aside from the pedestrian, but still necessary, slog of selling raffle tickets and knocking on doors for direct donations, the major thrust for the fundraising was a charity film show that I arranged to be held at the Cathay, Jesselton. It was a full-blown gala event, graced by the presence of the British Governor of North Borneo and his wife. The charity show cast the spotlight on a laudable cause that the Jesselton community responded to with generosity, and with the money raised, the construction of the facilities for the blind began on a seven acre plot of land about a half-an-hour drive north of Jesselton. Upon completion, the centre opened its doors under the banner of the Wallace Training Centre—in memory of an Englishman who was a respected eye surgeon at the Jesselton hospital.

In 1963, the combined efforts of the Rotary Club and the Red Cross Society enabled the North Borneo Royal Society of the Blind to be formed. Having completed my term as Rotary Club President in mid-1962, I agreed to assume the mantle of presidency for the Society for the Blind. I was also concurrently holding the post of vice president for the Red Cross Society. It was an extremely busy period but I had never been happier ... and a fool to think that it would last.

It was June 1964. North Borneo was now part of Malaysia—having merged with the Federation of Malaya, together with Sarawak and Singapore, in September 1963—and was renamed Sabah; Jesselton was now called Kota Kinabalu and the Red Cross would eventually become the Red Crescent. It was eight o'clock Sunday morning and the harsh jangle of the phone made me wonder who could be calling at such an early hour at the weekend. It was one of my mahjong partners. He asked whether I had heard the news.

I was puzzled. "What news?"

"Dato Loke is dead, plane crash yesterday. It's on the radio."

His words struck me like a bolt of lightning. I was aware that Dato Loke was attending a film festival in Taiwan but I couldn't believe that such a terrible thing had happened. I waited in trepidation for the nine o'clock news. There was tightness in my chest when I heard for myself the radio report about an air crash in Taiwan that had killed everyone onboard—Dato Loke had been one of the passengers.

I managed to phone through to the Cathay people in Singapore at ten o'clock, hoping that they could shed more light on the situation, but they were reeling from shock and confusion. It was only a few days later that Cathay issued an official statement to all key managers regarding Dato Loke's death; he had gone on an unplanned side-trip to Taichung with his wife and a number of Cathay personnel. It was a trip that had unfortunately ended in disaster.

Together with that announcement came orders to temporarily freeze the No 1 corporate account and that the No 2 accounts—under the names of the various cinema managers—were to be used to both settle operating expenses and salary payments, as well as deposit the daily takings. It fell upon me to convey this instruction to all the managers in my territory. This hasty re-arrangement was just the tip of the turmoil reverberating through the organisation, for Dato Loke's sudden and tragic demise had badly shaken the company. I wondered how long it would take before things returned to normal.

Meanwhile, there was an urgent re-assignment of personnel and responsibilities in an attempt to keep Cathay running on an even keel, and I was tasked to return to Singapore and assume the post of Deputy Manager of International Films Distributor Ltd, Singapore (later shortened to Cathay Films Distributors).

The transitory nature of my postings was an occupational hazard that I had learnt to accept in my career, but it was becoming more difficult to face it with the same panache of the early days, when all it had required was for me to stuff my clothes into my battered suitcase, fold up my camp bed and be on my way. It was not until my stint in Kuching that I had been sedentary enough to gather any moss. After having been ensconced in Jesselton (I still couldn't get used to calling it Kota Kinabalu) for twice as long, it was more than moss that clung to me, I was almost sessile.

Although those nine years seemed to flash by in the blink of an eye, it was a long time; long enough to see Jolly growing up along with his childhood friends and finish his primary schooling; long enough for me to become a prominent figure in the local landscape, and certainly long enough to make it to the Head of State's birthday honours list to receive the Ali Darjah Kinabalu (ADK)—an award for notable public services rendered to the State—at an official ceremony due in a couple of months. It didn't seem possible that I'd once been struggling to earn a living and lamenting the mediocrity of my existence. The anguish of those days was a reminder of how far I had come and how much I was now being asked to leave behind. It was not my choice to leave, but there could only be one response to the company's rallying call.

Two months after Dato Loke's death, I boarded a plane at Jesselton airport bound for Singapore. As I strapped in and waited for take-off, I thought of how my life had turned a full circle sixteen years later, with me heading back to work in Singapore where my adventures with Cathay had first started. My wife and younger son would follow after household and schooling matters had been taken care of. It was for the better. A race riot had broken out in Singapore the month before. Hundreds of people had been injured and there had been about two dozen fatalities. Although the curfew had been lifted, I felt more at ease that my family would be joining me a little later. The last time there had been riots in Singapore was in 1955 and 1956, and it was quite disturbing to see such social disorder rearing its ugly head again.

Casey was staying back as he was just beginning to carve out his career, but the lad would need to find his own accommodation as I intended to rent out the house. I had to proffer my sincere apologies to the state office for not being able to attend the Head of State's award ceremony. The short notice for my departure led to a flurry of farewell lunches and dinners thrown by colleagues, friends, clubs and associations. I felt like I was rushing from one meal to another in a food marathon. Amidst the camaraderie, handshakes and well-wishes, I could see the unspoken question in their eyes: "When are you coming back?" It was inconceivable to all those around me that I would not angle to return like a boomerang once this crisis had blown over. It was obvious that I belonged here. I was glad that the question remained unvoiced, for I didn't know how to unsheathe the truth from well-worn clichés to address their expectations. I thought about my father who had earned his living wandering from place to place, and found it ironic that I had ended up following his footsteps in a manner of speaking, except, of course, my father finally decided to settle down in one place and in so choosing declared himself the master of his own destiny.

Having taxied into position, the whine of the plane's engines rose to a harpy's scream that sent the aircraft hurtling down the runway at ever-increasing speed till the rushing air gripped its wings and lifted the trembling fuselage. There was the thump, thump of wheels being folded as the plane continued its ascent. I peered out of the window and watched the ground recede. In the distance was the unmistakable profile of Mount Kinabalu. Part of the Crocker range, it stands at over 13,000 feet above sea level and is one of the highest mountains in Southeast Asia. Despite its daunting height, it is said to be one of the easiest mountains in the world to climb, with no special skill or equipment needed. The mountain lies only eighty-five miles from the city and, in fact,

Dancing with the Kadazan girls in Sabah.

thousands of people undertake the two- to three-day expedition to its peak every year. I never did. I guess that some things are not meant to be, like striking out on my own for example; it just wasn't in me to be a hard-nosed entrepreneur so I never considered it. Neither was I a mountain climber. The plane banked and Kinabalu was lost from view.

Epilogue

The majesty of Gunung Kinabalu with its crown of clouds is matched by the simple charm of its cloak of myths. One such myth concerns a prince from China who was shipwrecked in Borneo. He fell madly in love with the daughter of one of the fishermen who had rescued him and married her. As the years passed, his marital bliss was disturbed by a growing restlessness, arising from homesickness and a desire to see his parents once more. He set off in a small sailing boat, promising to return with a grand fleet of ships to bring his wife and children back with him to China. Although his journey was perilous, he eventually made it home. His parents were overjoyed to see him—for they had given him up for dead—and there was great celebration and feasting. When they learnt of his intent to fetch his Borneo family, they were horrified and forbade him from doing so, reminding their son that he had already been betrothed to a princess of a neighbouring kingdom as part of a political alliance. His ineluctable duty as a royal prince and his filial obligation as an obedient son left him no choice. It was with great sadness that he shed his role as a husband and father by abandoning those who were waiting for him on an island far away. Back in Borneo, his native wife waited patiently.

Each day at sunrise, she would leave her village to climb to the top of the mountain so as to be the first to catch sight of ships appearing on the horizon, hoping that one of them carried her husband onboard. She would only return home at sunset when it became too dark to see. This went on for months, then years, until she finally died from cold and exhaustion. Touched by the woman's faithful devotion to her husband, the mountain spirit transformed her into a stone, her face turned in the direction of the South China Sea, so that she could forever continue to be on the lookout for her beloved's return.